Communication & Negotiation

By Peggy Berry, MBA, RAC

Copyright © 2011 by the Regulatory Affairs Professionals Society.

All rights reserved.

978-0-9829321-6-2

At the time of publication, all Internet references (URLs) in this book were valid. However, these references are subject to change without notice.

Book Design by Karol A. Keane, Keanedesign.com

Making better healthcare products possible^{sm}

5635 Fishers Lane
Suite 550
Rockville, MD 20852
USA

Tel +1 301 770 2920
Fax +1 301 770 2924

Washington, DC ▪ Brussels ▪ Tokyo

RAPS.org

About the Author

Peggy Berry, MBA, MFA, RAC, is vice president, regulatory affairs and quality at Amarin Corporation, responsible for the strategic management and oversight of the regulatory affairs, quality and pharmacovigilance departments. She has more than 20 years of experience in drug development and regulatory including senior level positions with Dyax Corp, AstraZeneca and Dey Pharmaceuticals and roles at two clinical contract research organizations (ILEX Oncology and Cato Research Ltd.) as well as project management work in review divisions at the US Food and Drug Administration. Berry also has consulted for companies such as emdSerono, Neurokos, Amgen and Biovex.

Table of Contents

Introduction 1

Chapter 1 The Basics of Communication 3
    Introduction 3
    Chapter Objectives 3
    Communication Basics 3
        Communication Models 5
            Aristotle's Model 5
            Berlo's Model 6
            Shannon and Weaver's Model 9
            Schramm's Model 10
            Helical Model 11
            Westley and McLean's Model 11
        The Communication Process 12
            Context 12
            Sender 12
            Message or Content 12
            Medium or Mode 13
            Receiver 13
            Feedback 13
    Communication Within an Organization 13
    Modes of Communication 14
        Oral Communication 14
            Advantages of Oral Communication 15
            Disadvantages/Limitations or Oral Communication 15
        Written Communication 16
            Advantages of Written Communication 16
            Disadvantages of Written Communication 17
    Communication vs. Effective Communication 17
    Barriers to Effective Communication 18
        Noise 19
        Unorganized or Disorganized Thoughts 20
        Wrong Interpretations 20
        Not Understanding the Receiver 20
        Ignoring the Content 20
        Avoiding the Listener or Receiver 21
        Not Confirming With the Receiver 21
        Low Volume and Tone 21
        Impatient Listener 21
        Personal Barriers 22

Table of Contents

Overcoming Barriers to Effective Communication 22
    Eliminate Differences in Perception 22
    Use Simple Language 22
    Employ Active Listening.. 22
    Consider Emotional State 23
    Avoid Information Overload 23
    Select Proper Mode/Medium... 23
Listening 23
Effective Communication in Meetings 24
    Step 1. Prepare.. 24
        What are your desired outcomes?..................................... 26
        Understand the Other Person's Perspective 26
    Step 2. Rehearse... 27
        Structure Your Thinking.. 27
    Step 3. Logistics 28
Chapter Summary 28

Chapter 2 Effective Communication in Practice............................... 31
Introduction 31
Chapter Objectives 31
Barriers to Effective Communication.. 31
        Noise or Environmental Distractions............................... 32
        Perception 32
        Stress, Emotional State and Time Pressure 32
        Message.. 32
        Ourselves... 33
        Culture or Bias 33
        Organizational Issues.. 34
Overcoming Communication Barriers 34
Noise or Environmental Distractions 34
Perception.. 34
Stress, Emotional State and Time Pressure..................................... 34
Message 34
Ourselves 35
Culture or Bias 35
Organizational Issues 35
        Active Listening... 36
Feedback 38
Effective Communication 38
    Completeness... 38

v

Table of Contents

Conciseness... 38
Consideration 39
Clarity... 39
Concreteness... 39
Courtesy.. 39
Correctness 39
Effective Communication at Work... 39
    Communication Flows in an Organization 40
        Downward 40
        Upward... 41
        Lateral.. 41
        Diagonal 42
        External 42
    Teamwork 43
    Team Development 43
        Stage 1: Forming 43
        Stage 2: Storming 44
        Stage 3: Norming 44
        Stage 4: Performing 45
            Scenario 1 45
            Scenario 2 46
    Team Management 46
        1. Do not interrupt.. 47
        2. Do not jump to conclusions. 48
        3. Do not judge the messenger. 48
            How the speaker sounds 49
            How the speaker looks 49
            The speaker's age 49
            Put yourself in the speaker's place 49
        4. Do not be self-centered. 50
        5. Do not tune out. 50
    Meetings 50
        Planning an Agenda 52
        People and Preparation 52
        Conducting the Meeting 53
        Meeting Follow-up 53
    Virtual Meetings 53
    Chapter Summary 54

Table of Contents

Chapter 3 Oral and Behavioral Communication 57
   Introduction 57
   Chapter Objectives 57
   Oral Communication 57
      Semiformal Oral Communication 58
      Formal Oral Communication... 62
         Preparing to Speak 62
            Know the purpose or objective of your presentation. 62
            Know your audience and what they already know. 63
            What should they know at the end of the communication?.. 63
            What content does it take to bridge the gap? 64
            Rehearse. 65
         Delivering the Presentation.. 65
         Conquering Your Fear of Public Speaking...................................... 66
            Enlist the help and support of the audience......................... 67
            Make your stage fright work for you...................................... 67
            Be confident; be prepared. 68
      Nonverbal Communication/Body Language 68
      Giving Feedback 69
      Chapter Summary... 70

Chapter 4 Written Communication 73
   Introduction 73
   Chapter Objectives 73
   Goals of Writing... 74
      Completeness, Consideration and Courtesy 75
         Questions to Consider About Your Readers.................................... 75
      Conciseness... 76
      Clarity.. 77
      Concreteness... 78
      Correctness 78
   Writing Emails 80
   Regulatory Writing.. 81
   Review and Proofread Your Document 82
   Improving Writing Skills 83
   Chapter Summary... 83

Table of Contents

Chapter 5 Influencing and Negotiating 87
    Introduction 87
    Chapter Objectives 88
    Influencing 88
        The Art of Persuasion 88
        Principles of Influence... 89
        Effective Influencing 89
            Tactic 1: Liking 90
            Tactic 2: Reciprocity 90
            Tactic 3: Social Proof 90
            Tactic 4: Consistency 91
            Tactic 5: Authority... 91
            Tactic 6: Scarcity 91
            Tactic 7: Indirect Influence 91
                Tactic 7a: Modeling and Matching.. 91
                Tactic 7b: Acting in Accord 91
                Tactic 7c: Reframing 91
                Tactic 7d: Paradox.. 92
                Tactic 7e: Confusion 92
                Tactic 7f: The Columbo Approach 92
                Tactic 7g: Storytelling and Metaphor 92
                Tactic 7h: Humor 92
    Negotiation.. 93
        Types of Negotiations.. 93
            Day-to-Day Negotiation... 94
            Contractual Negotiation.. 94
            Legal Negotiation 95
        Negotiation Models 95
            Win-Win Model 95
            Win-Lose and Lose-Win Models... 96
            Lose-Lose Model 96
            RADPAC Model 96
    Challenges to Effective Negotiation 97
    Negotiation Skills 98
    The Negotiation Process.. 99
        Planning.. 99
        Communicating 101
        Developing Solutions.. 103
        Closing 103
    Negotiation Styles 104

Table of Contents

    1. Collaboration 104
    2. Accommodation 104
    3. Competition 105
    4. Conflict Avoidance 105
    5. Compromise 105
  Difficult Tactics 105
  Chapter Summary 106

Chapter 6 Global Business Etiquette and Cultural Considerations 109
  Introduction 109
  Chapter Objectives 109
  Cultural Awareness 109
  Diversity in an Organization 110
  Intercultural Communication Across an Organization 111
  Intercultural Communication Outside an Organization 112
  Conduct Research 112
    Business Care Etiquette 112
    Holidays 113
    Professional Titles 113
    Greeting 113
    Gift-giving and Receiving 114
    Body Language 114
    Other Common Practices and Etiquette 114
  General Intercultural Communication Strategies 115
  Cross-cultural Negotiations 116
  Chapter Summary 116

Exercise and Quiz Answers 119

Introduction

Introduction

Imagine a world without communication. You have a brilliant idea but you cannot tell anyone because you do not have the power of communication. You have a strong desire for something, but cannot express your desires. Life would be dull, gray and lonely. Communication is a necessity.

Communication and its subset, negotiation, are essential skills for any professional whose work may require influencing others. For regulatory professionals, these skills become critical since their responsibilities regularly include negotiations with global regulatory agencies and/or Notified Bodies/Registrars and discussions with corporate management internally or at partner companies. Effective communication is also important during due diligence when working with project teams.

This book provides a basic description of communication and negotiation skills and their importance throughout all regulatory activities, both internal and external. It explores how to communicate and negotiate more effectively in all interactions, including interviews, presentations and meetings.

Learning Objectives
- Define "communication," "negotiation" and associated terminology.
- Outline the basics and critical elements of effective communication.
- Explain the major negotiation process phases.

Target Audience

This is an introductory book designed for regulatory professionals interested in learning the basics of effective communication and negotiation.

Communication and Negotiation

Chapter 1
The Basics of Communication

Introduction
Talking is not the same thing as communicating. Talking is speaking out loud at another person, creating the illusion that communication has occurred. However, communication is more complicated.

Have you ever been in a meeting and later heard another attendee speaking about the discussion that took place, only to think to yourself: "That's not what we talked about!" Perhaps that attendee was only listening to herself.

Communication is the process of creating shared understanding. This process comprises exchanging ideas or thoughts with others, hearing, understanding and comprehending them and then articulating them to confirm that everyone heard and understood the same information. There are three basic types of communication: written, spoken and nonverbal.

Communication is more than just the words you say or the documents you write. Actions speak louder than words.

Chapter Objectives
- Define the communication process.
- Identify the major communication methods.
- Identify how to make communication effective.

Communication Basics
"Communication" is defined as the "imparting or interchange of thought, opinions, or information by speech, writing, or signs."[1] Or, as a process by which we assign and convey meaning in an attempt to create shared understanding.[2]

This process requires a vast repertoire of skills in listening, observing, speaking, questioning, analyzing and evaluating. Use of these processes spans all areas of life: home, community, workplace and beyond. It is through communication that collaboration and cooperation occur.

Communication and Negotiation

"Communication is not a skill. It is the skill."

— *Harry Beckwith*

Communication requires a sender, a message and one or more intended recipients. Communication can occur across vast distances in time and space. The communication process is complete once the receiver has understood the sender's message.

Nonverbal communication is the process of conveying meaning in the form of non-word messages. Nonverbal communication includes gestures, body language, posture, facial expression and eye contact. Nonverbal communication also includes personal attributes such as clothing, hairstyle and tone of voice.

Communication in the workplace is ubiquitous and the skill of communicating well is highly sought after by employers. Unfortunately, most of us are not very good at communicating our knowledge, and the results can be disastrous.[3]

"Eighty-five percent of failures in quality are failures in communication."
— *W. Edwards Deming, the 20th century's leading advocate for "quality" as a business goal*

A big part of the problem is the way we think about communication. Too often, we make assumptions that everyone is a skilled communicator or that individuals understand more about the topic than they do.

Communication is essential for all aspects of life. David Newkirk and Stuart Crainer wrote that "perhaps the most important lesson from the Iraq war is that managing real-time communications is as important as managing real-time processes. Communication is moving from being a peripheral, specialist responsibility to being an essential and integral element of corporate leadership."[4] Similarly, central to all five recommendations of the 9/11 Commission was the need for improved communication.

Pay attention to the actual results of your speaking and writing. Figure out what communication strategies work for you and what strategies do not. Notice when you are understood and when you are not. If you are not sure that you have been understood, actively seek feedback from the receiver.

"There is one thing worse than not communicating. It is thinking you have communicated when you have not."

— Edgar Dale, American educator

Read and listen to communication from cultures and countries other than your own. In Chapter 6, you will learn an approach to communicating across cultures. In addition, occasionally pick up issues of unfamiliar magazines or spend a few minutes with a cable channel from another culture. You will broaden your knowledge and enhance your communication techniques.

Make sure that your communication process is as efficient and effective as possible. That is what this book is about, of course—making your speaking, writing and nonverbal communication processes more specific, streamlined and effective.

Start collecting tools that describe effective communication methods and techniques from various sources. You will find some powerful tools in this book as well as the cited references. But, also start your own file on effective communication. For example, if you receive a particularly good email or letter, save it. If you hear a powerful, inspirational or persuasive speech, take notes about what makes it so great. You will soon be filling your own toolbox with useful ideas and models.

Communication Models

Models are widely used to depict an idea or concept in a way that makes the concept clearer for easier learning. Following is a review of several communication models.

Aristotle's Model

Aristotle was the first to design a communication model. In this model, the speaker, or sender, plays the key role in the communication. The sender takes complete charge of the communication. He prepares the content, carefully crafting his thoughts into words with the objective of influencing the receiver, who is then expected to respond in the sender's desired way. The content has to be impressive for the receiver to be influenced and respond accordingly.

One example of this type of communication is a political meeting where the prospective leader delivers a speech in an attempt to gain votes by trying to persuade the constituency that he will be able to solve problems that are important to them. He must deliver his speech in a manner that will motivate the receivers to cast their votes in his favor, or in other words, respond in the manner that the speaker desires. Here, the sender is the center of attention and the receivers are passive.

The sender must carefully select the words and content of the message based on an understanding of his target audience. When delivering his speech, he should make eye contact with the receivers. His vocal tone and pitch should be loud and clear enough for the people to hear and understand the speech properly. Voice modulation plays an important role in creating the desired effect. Similar pitch throughout the speech makes it monotonous and minimizes its impact. The speaker should know which words should receive more stress and where to pause, emphasize or exaggerate to influence the listeners.

Aristotle's model of communication is widely accepted and the most commonly used method. It is used in public speaking, seminars and lectures where the sender makes his points clear by designing influential content and confidently delivering the message to the receivers, with the expectation that they will respond accordingly. As mentioned, the sender is active and the receiver is passive.

Berlo's Model

In David Berlo's model of communication, the emotional aspect of the message is taken into account. Berlo's model of communication operates on the SMCRD model, where each letter stands for one of the aspects of communication.
1. an information *source*, which produces a message
2. a transmitter, which encodes the *message* into signals
3. a *channel*, to which signals are adapted for transmission
4. a *receiver*, which "decodes" (reconstructs) the message from the signal
5. a *destination*, where the message arrives

Source

The source or the sender is where the message originates. She is the one who transfers the message to the receiver. The source or sender transfers her information to the receiver using communication skills, attitude, knowledge, social system and culture.

Communication Skills

An individual must possess excellent communication skills to make her communication effective and create an impact among the listeners. The speaker must know where to take pauses, where to repeat a sentence, how to emphasize a particular sentence, etc. The speaker should also make a point to check in with the audience and listen to their questions.

Attitude

If you have the right attitude you can be quite influential. A person might be a good speaker but if she does not have the right attitude, she would not be effective. The right attitude will create a good and lasting impression on the listeners. Generally, the right attitude is an attitude that is positive, inspirational and encouraging.

Knowledge

In this model, knowledge is not related to the speaker's educational qualifications or the number of degrees she has. Rather, it is the clarity of the information she wants to convey to the listener. The speaker must have thorough, in-depth knowledge about the subject of the message.

Social System

A speaker must be aware of the social system in the area where she is speaking. For example, if a politician delivered a speech where she proposes constructing a Jewish Temple in an area primarily populated by Muslims, the reaction will not likely be a positive one and she will fail to persuade her audience. The displeasure of the audience is because the speaker ignored the social environment in which she was communicating. She disregarded the sentiments, beliefs and religious feelings of the receivers.

Culture

Culture refers to the cultural background of the receivers of the message.

Message

When a sender converts her thoughts into words, a message is created. A message comprises the following elements:

Content

No one can read your mind to know what you are thinking. Your thought has to be put into words and content has to be prepared around it.

Content is the script of the message. The content has to be understandable, accurate and impactful so the receiver will be persuaded.

Elements (or Gestures)

It has been observed that speech alone cannot create the most impactful communication. It is also important to incorporate hand movements, gestures, facial expressions and other body movements to capture the attention of the listener. These are the elements of the message.

Treatment

Treatment means the way the sender treats the message and conveys it to the receivers. The sender must understand the message's importance to the receiver and must know how to handle it. For example, if a boss needs to fire an employee, he should be authoritative and serious, and not express his message in a casual way.

Structure

A message needs to be properly structured to convey it in the most effective form. Often, this is in the most logical order, e.g., from beginning to end.

Code

In the same way that the correct code is required to open a combination lock, the code in communication has to be correct. Your body movements, language, expressions and gestures (the elements) have to be accurate to or in accordance with the spoken words or the message will be distorted and the recipient will not be able to decode and understand it.

Channel

Channel refers to the medium, or the way in which the information flows from the sender to the receiver. Here, the senses are the channels. For example, when you speak, your message is received through hearing or when you read or get a message from pictures, you receive it through seeing. All five senses are channels that help us communicate with one another.

Receiver

When the message reaches the receiver, he tries to understand what the sender is trying to convey with the message and respond or react accordingly.

This is also called decoding after the message has arrived at its destination.

Destination

There are limitations to Berlo's model of communication. For example, the speaker and the listener must be on common ground (e.g., understand much of the same background, be of the same mindset, etc.) for smooth communication, which is not always practical.

Shannon and Weaver's Model

The Shannon and Weaver model is the most popular model of communication and is widely accepted all over the world. As with the above models, the Shannon and Weaver model suggests that a message originates from the person who gets the thought or has the information. This person is the sender or the source of information. The information is then transmitted from the brain to the mouth and comes out as a signal that reaches the recipient after moving through several noises and other disturbances. The recipient then passes the message to its final destination, other individuals.

Shannon and Weaver argued that there were three levels of problems for communication.
- The technical problem: how accurately can the message be transmitted?
- The semantic problem: how precisely is the meaning conveyed?
- The effectiveness problem: how effectively does the received meaning affect behavior?

Peter is a regulatory vice president with a global pharmaceutical company. Mike reports to Peter and has a small team working for him. Peter wanted Mike to prepare a thorough report on a product's regulatory strategy that could be used to achieve the goals of the organization. He also wanted a detailed study on the competitor's strategy by the end of the day. While Peter was speaking to Mike, they were interrupted by the administrator who was taking lunch orders for a noon meeting. Finally, when Mike received the rest of the message, he returned to his department and delegated the responsibility to his team members. Mike tried to convey what Peter expected the team to prepare. At the end of the day, the team prepared a report and submitted it to Peter. Upon review, Peter found that there were some errors.

Peter is the source of information. He shared his thoughts as a message to Mike through speaking. In this model, Peter's mouth is the transmitter, which helps in relaying the message. His voice is the signal being sent to Mike about what he is expected to do. Without signal or content, Mike would not know what he is supposed to do.

When the conversation was interrupted by the person taking the lunch order, the signals were interrupted, causing possible distortion on the way to the receiver. Noises come from many sources causing distractions to the communicators or possibly distorting the message.

In this example, the team prepared the report but there were some errors that had to be corrected. This is the limitation of the Shannon and Weaver model. The message, while reaching the final destination, may be distorted, causing the message to be interpreted differently. Even a simple message can take on a different meaning on its way to the final destination.

Schramm's Model

Schramm's model of communication has its roots in the Shannon and Weaver model. This model suggests that information is of no use unless and until it is put into words and conveyed to others. Encoding plays a very important role because it initiates the process of communication by converting the thought into content of the message. When the information reaches the receiver, it is her responsibility to understand what the speaker is trying to convey. Unless and until the receiver is able to understand or decode the message, it is of no use. Thus, in this model, encoding and decoding are the two most important factors of effective communication.

This model also emphasizes that the communication is incomplete if the sender has not gotten feedback from the recipient. The Schramm model suggests that communication is a two-way process between the sender and the receiver; whenever the information reaches the recipient, it becomes her responsibility to give feedback to the sender that she has understood the message. If the receiver is not clear about something, she must request clarification from the speaker.

Schramm believed that an individual's knowledge, experience and cultural background also play an important role in communication. Individuals from diverse cultures, religions or backgrounds tend to interpret the message in different ways. One reason for this is denotative and connotative meanings.

Denotative meaning comes from the definition of words. It is almost the same for all individuals who have learned to speak a language, including non-native speakers, because it comes from a dictionary, language book or similar learning or reference source. Because of this common reference, denotative meaning has a lower chance of misinterpretation and misunderstanding than connotative meanings. However, denotative meanings can cause misinterpretation if words are used that are less common, more technical, have several possible meanings or have different meanings if they are used in a different context or different region.

Connotative meaning is a further implied or receiver-interpreted meaning placed on words or phrases that is affected by emotional factors, attitude, context and cultural circumstances. The connotative meaning can also be influenced by body movements, gestures, facial expressions and other factors. The connotative meaning is harder for the sender to control because some of the influencing factors may be unknown. However, having a good understanding of the receiver will allow for some control over connotative meaning.

Helical Model

Another model of communication is the Helical Model, which was proposed by Frank Dance in 1967. Dance thought of the communication process as similar to a helix.

A helix is a smooth curve just like a spring that, if it goes up, also comes down. According to this model, the process of communication evolves from birth and continues throughout life.

The model suggests that the communication process, just like a helix, moves forward as well as backward and is dependent upon the behavior patterns of the past with some modifications and changes. For example, as a child grows up, she makes some changes in her body movements or pronunciation or facial expressions. She makes certain modifications in her communication and tries to get rid of past communication errors. Overall, the communication process evolves for an individual but many of the things she has learned are retained.

Westley and MacLean's Model

The Westley and MacLean model of communication was proposed in 1957 by Bruce Westley and Malcolm S. MacLean, Jr. This model suggests that communication does not start with sending but actually begins when the speaker receives signals or messages from his external surroundings.

Hence, communication actually starts with receipt of a message from the environment, for example, when you see a car accident and you call the police, communication was initiated because of the accident.

In this model it is not necessary that the signals coming from external surroundings be intentionally sent; sometimes events might accidentally occur or the thought could be accidentally received. Thus, signals can be received anytime and communication can begin anytime.

The Communication Process

A review of all of the communication models reveals similar components, although they may be called by different names. The main components of communication process are:

Context

Communication is affected by the context in which it takes place. This may be physical, social, chronological or cultural. Every communication has a context. The sender chooses the message to communicate and, to the best extent possible, should also choose the appropriate context within which to present the message to enhance its understanding and acceptance. If a choice is not made by the sender, the context will still impact the message and it may be less effective or influential than it otherwise would have been. For example, if a wife wants to have a discussion with her husband about taking an expensive family holiday, the best context would not be while he is watching a sporting event on television. She will have a more receptive and influential communication if she waits until she can have his full attention.

Sender

The sender is the person who sends the message. A sender makes use of words, pictures, visual aids and nonverbal communication to convey the message and try to produce the required response. The sender may be an individual, a group or an organization.

The sender's views, background, approach, skills, competencies and knowledge have an impact on the message.

Message or Content

The message is an idea that the sender wants to communicate. The verbal and nonverbal content chosen are essential to ensure the message is interpreted by the receiver as intended by the sender.

Medium or Mode

The medium is the means used to exchange or transmit the message. The sender must choose a medium, i.e., speech, writing, by which to convey the message. The choice of appropriate medium of communication is essential for the communication to be effective and accurately interpreted.

Receiver

The receiver is the person or people for whom the message is intended. The degree to which the receiver understands the message is dependent upon various factors such as knowledge, emotional state, context and distractions.

Feedback

Feedback is the component of the communication process that permits the sender to know whether the message was properly received and interpreted. Feedback may be verbal or nonverbal (in the form of smiles, sighs, facial expressions, etc.). It may also take written form such as memos, reports, responses or surveys.

"No one would talk much in society if they knew how often they misunderstood others."   — *Johann Wolfgang Von Goethe*

In summary, communication is a process of exchanging verbal, written and nonverbal messages. It is a continuous process. The prerequisite of communication is a message. This message must be conveyed through some medium to the receiver. Communication is successful when the message is correctly understood by the receiver as intended by the sender. The receiver must respond with feedback. Communication is incomplete without feedback from the receiver to the sender on how well the message is understood.

Communication Within an Organization

Communication is an important skill within an organization. It is essential for leaders and managers so they can perform the basic functions of management, including planning, organizing, giving assignments and other responsibilities. And, it is essential for all employees so they can share their ideas, understand their managers and co-workers and perform their jobs well.

The importance of communication within an organization can be summarized as follows:

- Communication motivates by informing employees about the task to be done, the manner in which they are to perform the task and how to improve their performance if it is not up to expected standards.
- Communication is a source of information to employees for the decision-making process.
- Communication plays a role in altering individuals' attitudes; for example, a well-informed employee generally has a better attitude than one who is less informed. Organizational magazines, emails, company meetings and other forms of communication help shape employee attitudes and behaviors.
- Communication helps in socializing and building relationships with co-workers.
- Communication also assists in controlling processes through various levels of hierarchy and establishing certain principles and guidelines employees must follow in an organization. They must comply with organizational policies, perform their job roles as expected and communicate any work problems and grievances to their manager.

A primary responsibility of a manager or leader within an organization is to develop and maintain an effective communication system. An effective and efficient communication system requires managerial proficiency in sending and receiving messages. A manager must identify any barriers to communication (see below) and take steps to avoid or overcome those barriers.

Modes of Communication
Oral Communication

Oral communication, while primarily referring to spoken verbal communication, typically relies on words, visual aids and nonverbal elements to convey the message. Oral communication includes discussions, speeches, presentations and interpersonal communication. In face-to-face communication, body language and voice tone play a role in the understanding of the message.

A great presenter must capture the attention of the audience and connect with them. For example, if two people tell the same joke, one may greatly amuse the audience due to his body language and tone of voice while the second, using exactly the same words, bores and irritates the audience. Visual aids can also help facilitate effective communication and are almost always used in presentations for an audience.

Oral communication is generally recommended when the matter being communicated is of a temporary nature or where a direct interaction is required. Face-to-face communication (meetings, lectures, conferences, interviews, etc.) is helpful to build rapport and trust.

Advantages of Oral Communication

- There is a high level of understanding and transparency in oral communication since it is interpersonal.
- There is no element of rigidity in oral communication. There is flexibility, allowing changes in previous decisions.
- The feedback is spontaneous. Thus, decisions can be made quickly without any delay.
- Oral communication is time-saving and may also save money.
- Oral communication is best for problem solving. Conflicts, disagreements and potential misunderstandings can be discussed and resolved.
- Oral communication contributes to group energy and is great for teamwork.
- Oral communication promotes good relationships among employees.
- Oral communication is best for conveying private and confidential information.

Disadvantages/Limitations of Oral Communication

- Relying only on oral communication may not be sufficient for all business communication, much of which is required to be formal and organized.
- Oral communication is time-saving as far as daily interactions go, but long speeches in meetings consume a lot of time and can be unproductive.
- Oral communications are not easy to retain and are therefore unreliable for future reference.
- There may be misunderstandings as the information is not complete and may lack essential parts.

- It requires attentiveness and receptivity on part of the receivers.
- Oral communication (such as speeches) is infrequently used as a legal record.

Written Communication

Written communication involves any kind of communication by means of written symbols. It relies on words, pictures, symbols and graphics to convey the message. Written communication includes letters, memos, reports, email, signs and visual aids used in presentations. In written communication, the careful choice of words, their organization in a specific order into sentences and cohesive compilation into paragraphs are vitally important because there is no nonverbal body language or voice tone to help the reader understand the message, and feedback to the writer is not immediate.

A great writer must be precise, factual and correct, above all else, because the written communication may be referenced in the future. Writing for promotion or presentation requires that the messages and their graphics capture the audience's attention and cause audience members to want to know more and stay engaged, leading to the desired behavior. Meeting minutes must be specific, precise and factual so future reference to what occurred can be accurate and helpful. See Chapter 4 for additional information about business writing.

Written communication is generally recommended when the information must be referenced or relied upon in the future. This includes documentation of oral communication as well as reports of studies and other materials submitted to regulatory agencies.

Advantages of Written Communication
- Written communication helps set forth an organization's principles, policies and rules.
- It is a permanent means of communication.
- It assists in proper delegation of responsibilities. In contrast, oral communication can lead to misunderstandings about the delegation of responsibilities.
- Written communication is more precise and explicit than oral communication.
- It provides ready records and references.
- It can be used to communicate to people outside the local organization or area.

- Legal matters can depend upon written communication as valid records.

Disadvantages of Written Communication
- Written communication does not receive immediate feedback or response.
- Written communication is time-consuming to prepare because it requires a certain precision for clarity.
- Effective written communication requires skills and competencies in language and vocabulary use. Poor writing skills and quality have a negative impact on the sender and/or the organization.
- Excessive paperwork and email add to employee workloads.

Communication vs. Effective Communication

When communicating, the more precise, concise and crisp the content, the more effective the communication.

It is essential for the sender to select and use correct, accurate words and phrases that the target audience will understand. The sender must first be clear about the communication's desired result (e.g., a decision, an agreement, etc.), the receiver of the message (e.g., management, peers, regulatory agency) and the message that must be conveyed to bring about action by the receivers.

"I want a drink," is *communication*.

"Would you please bring me a glass of iced tea from the clear pitcher," is *effective communication*.

When thinking of effective communication versus communication, I am reminded of the movie "When Harry Met Sally." In this movie, there are several scenes during which Harry and Sally are ordering from restaurant menus. Harry always chooses something directly off of the menu—he communicates his choice to the waiter, e.g., "a glass of water and a Caesar salad with chicken, please." Sally, on the other hand, never chooses directly from the menu. Rather, she personalizes her choice to be precisely what she wants, e.g., "a glass of water in a real glass, not a plastic glass, with three ice cubes, and one slice of lemon on the side—not the side of the glass but in a dish on the side; and a Caesar salad with well-done but not crispy grilled chicken, no croutons and no anchovies, one extra spoonful of Parmesan cheese, and fat-free Caesar dressing on the side."

To me, this sums up how effective communication works. The sender of the message must know exactly what she wants to occur and what the message content must be to enable the receiver to appropriately respond and bring about the desired action or outcome.

This requires the choice of precise, accurate words and an appropriate level of detail to gain the desired result, all arranged in an organized and understandable manner so the receiver can comprehend it. In the example above, if Sally orders her meal in a haphazard way, it is likely that something will not be done correctly. For example, "a glass of water with lemon and ice and a Caesar salad with chicken and fat-free dressing; make sure that the lemon and dressing are on the side. Oh, and just three ice cubes; no anchovies. And, I want the chicken well done but not crispy and extra Parmesan cheese. And a real glass, no plastic, and no croutons, either." Presenting information in an illogical, haphazard manner will cause the person taking the order to be unable to follow the communication clearly and misunderstand or become confused about what Sally really wants.

Effective communication is also created specifically for the target audience. In other words, when you know what action or result you want, you generally know who is going to take that action. This person or these people are your target audience—the receiver(s) of the message. It is important that you understand who they are (e.g., age, education, experience), what they already know about your message topic and what they need to know to deliver your desired result. To illustrate this further, complete Exercise 1.1 on the following page.

Communication passes information to a receiver. Effective communication passes a precise and accurate message to a receiver and ensures that the receiver understands the message as it was intended. Effective communication allows work to be accomplished with fewer errors and in a shorter span of time. It also minimizes misunderstandings, conflicts and errors that can occur from an unclear or unorganized message.

Barriers to Effective Communication

Imagine a situation where you ask your team members for a report that needs to be forwarded to the organization's managing director. What if your team misinterprets your information, bungles the project and fails to submit it by the deadline? The managing director will make your life

> **Exercise 1.1. Writing for the Target Audience**
>
> You are an experienced regulatory affairs manager at a mid-sized pharmaceutical company. You have been in this career for about 10 years and you love the work that you do. Your primary responsibility is to review labeling and advertising materials for one of your company's product lines. Your 17-year-old daughter asks you to speak at career day for her senior high school class and you agree. Your presentation is expected to last between five and seven minutes.
>
> What is the desired outcome of this communication? What do you know about your target audience and how will this shape your message? What do you need to tell your audience in order to achieve the desired outcome? Draft your two-minute introduction.
>
> See page 119 for the way I would complete this exercise. What do you think of my answers?

miserable. The poor communication could actually cost you your job.

Communication barriers are the obstacles and hurdles that arise in during a communication and lead to misunderstandings and misinterpretations by the receiver. Barriers to effective communication can distort the message so it is not received and understood by the receiver as intended. It is critically important to overcome barriers so effective communication can occur.

Following is a discussion of common communication barriers.

Noise

Noise from any source can be a major barrier to effective communication. If you are trying to send a message to someone and you are standing next to a speaker with blaring music, do you think the receiver will be able to interpret the message correctly? Because of the noise, the message will never reach the receiver as intended. Any presentation or speech delivered in a noisy room is pointless because the information is either not heard or is distorted. It is the sender's responsibility to ensure the message is delivered under the best circumstances, including a noise-free environment. If the sender has not fulfilled this responsibility, it becomes the receiver's responsibility to inform the sender that the message cannot or is not being received and must be delivered in a noise-free environment.

Unorganized or Disorganized Thoughts

Unorganized or disorganized thoughts lead to poor communication. It is the sender's responsibility to organize his thoughts in a logical manner so they can be conveyed clearly to the receiver. If the sender does not fulfill this responsibility, it becomes the receiver's responsibility to ask questions, provide feedback and try to understand the message or inform the sender that it cannot be understood.

Wrong Interpretations

Wrong interpretations cause a misunderstanding of the message and are a barrier to effective communication. Wrong interpretations can occur if words have more than one meaning and the sender's message is not understood by the receiver with the intended meaning. This type of miscommunication is prone to occur with language and cultural differences where words can have different meanings. It is the receiver's responsibility to give proper feedback to the speaker to confirm that the message has been understood. As the receiver, if you are not clear about anything in the communication, it is important to ask. If the receiver does not provide feedback to the sender, it becomes the sender's responsibility to seek feedback from the receiver(s) to ensure the message was communicated and understood as intended.

Not Understanding the Receiver

It is important that the receiver be targeted by the sender. The sender should not just prepare a speech. She needs to learn more about the listeners' culture, habits and thought processes. The sender must first understand the receiver and then determine how best to communicate the message. Failing to understand the receiver is a barrier to effective communication. It is the sender's responsibility to understand the receiver's perspective and deliver the message in the way it will be best understood. If the sender does not fulfill this responsibility, it becomes the receiver's responsibility to attempt to understand the message through questions and clarifications or to inform the sender that the message is not being understood in its current content or context.

Ignoring the Content

A major part of communication is the content of the message. The message's content has to be clear, crisp, interesting and focused. Make sure the content is relevant. When delivering a speech, use interesting words and stories so you also entertain your listeners. Understand your content and try to make it more interesting and relevant. It is the sender's responsibility to ensure the message's content is not ignored. If the sender does not fulfill this responsibility, the receiver can attempt to understand the message through questions.

Avoiding the Listener or Receiver

If you attend a seminar and the speaker is reading from his notes and not making eye contact with you or anyone else, it will be difficult to relate to him or to understand his message. Not connecting with the listener is a barrier to effective communication. If you are the speaker or the message sender, make sure you create a friendly atmosphere before you start communicating. Be familiar with your topic so you do not have to read your notes and are able to make eye contact with the listeners.

Not Confirming With the Receiver

Getting feedback that the message has been received is critical to effective communication. When communicating orally, it is important to check with the listeners to make sure they have received the message as it was intended. If the message was not received correctly, it should be clarified, restated or otherwise corrected. You can improve message clarity when speaking by pausing at appropriate times, spelling out difficult words and defining words that are more complex. When communicating in writing, it is more difficult to confirm with the receiver, so it is important to ensure that the message is clear and understandable. It is the sender's responsibility to confirm with the receiver and the receiver's responsibility to provide feedback to the sender.

Low Volume and Tone

If you are speaking and the listeners cannot hear you, effective communication is impossible. The content can be accurate, crisp and relevant but if it does not reach the listeners, they will not be able to understand it. Make sure you speak loudly enough for those in the last row to hear you, or use a microphone that will reach them. As a listener, if you are unable to hear the speaker, do not be afraid to provide feedback and ask the person to speak more loudly.

Impatient Listener

If the listener does not take enough time to hear and understand the full message, the communication cannot be effective. As a sender, it is important to recognize when the listener is not willing or available to hear the message and to arrange a better time to send it.

Personal Barriers

An individual's personal barriers to communication can be caused by personal stress, pressure, rivalry, low self-esteem, unhealthy competition, personal difficulties, biases and so on. It is each individual's responsibility to be aware of these barriers to communication and to overcome them so they may effectively send and receive messages.

Overcoming Barriers to Effective Communication

To ensure effective communication occurs, it is essential to recognize and deal with communication barriers. The previous section discussed barriers to communication, including responsibilities of the message sender and receiver about how to deal with those specific communication barriers. In addition to those responsibilities, following are several tactics to use for overcoming barriers to effective communication.

Eliminate Differences in Perception

Get to know the target audience, understand their perspective about the message and try to bridge the gap between their perception and your message to achieve the desired outcome.

Use Simple Language

Use of simple, clear words is most effective in all communication settings. Do not use ambiguous words, slang or profanity. Also, be aware when you are using industry jargon, corporate jargon or acronyms, i.e., terminology that your industry or company has coined and may not be shared by other companies even in the same industry. Another pitfall is regional slang or idioms.

Employ Active Listening

Active listening is the responsibility of both the message sender and the receiver. Listen attentively and carefully. Active listening means hearing with proper understanding of the message, asking clarifying questions and providing feedback to the message sender. As the sender, active listening will attune you to the potential misinterpretation or misunderstanding by the receiver(s) and allow you to clarify the message with more-precise or -accurate wording.

Consider Emotional State

During communication, the emotional state (e.g., stress, anger, irritation, etc.) of the sender or receiver may affect the communication. Make an attempt to overcome these potential barriers within yourself. If you are communicating with someone who is in a difficult emotional state, exercise empathy and exhibit a greater degree of patience with them so the communication can be effective.

Avoid Information Overload

Employees must be able to prioritize their work and focus on the important tasks that need to be done rather than overload themselves with work that has limited value. If it is difficult to prioritize work due to unclear communication or too much information or if the priorities are too great to accomplish within the expected period of time, it is important to bring this to the attention of your supervisor so the situation can be resolved before it becomes a problem.

Select Proper Mode/Medium

Choose the proper mode or medium of communication for your message and desired outcome. As discussed above, simple messages can be effectively conveyed orally in one-on-one interactions or meetings. And, written communication should be used for delivering messages that are complicated or need to be recalled precisely or distributed beyond those involved in the immediate communication.

Listening

Listening is a communication skill that is often overlooked. Most people learn to read and write in school, but are not generally taught how to listen. It has been estimated, however, that we spend at least 45% of our work time listening (or supposedly listening). Perhaps due to lack of training in listening, individuals do not hear everything that is being said to them. Another problem is being distracted by thinking about other things. When we do not listen carefully, we often fill in those gaps with our own assumptions.

Take, for example, the story of a manager at a contract research organization (CRO) who needed a document rushed through in 24 hours so her best customer could have it for an urgent US Food and Drug

Administration (FDA) meeting. She gave careful instructions about the project to the person who would write the document but, before she could finish, the writer had already stopped listening. As a result, he assumed that the manager wanted the document in three days, which was the usual deadline for most of these documents. When the manager went to get the document the next day, it was not ready. The deadline was missed and the company almost lost the customer. Unfortunately, stories like these are common in many organizations.

Being a good listener involves actively paying attention to the message sender and gaining an understanding of that message. If the message is not clear or requires further information, an active listener will ask questions and provide other feedback to the sender until the message is understood. See Chapter 2 for a more detailed discussion on active listening.

Effective Communication in Meetings

In today's corporate culture, meetings are a common method for communicating and decision making. Cross-functional teams are expected to work and make decisions collaboratively, and meetings are the primary forums for accomplishing many of their tasks. Therefore, team members must all be able to speak and write clearly so others can understand them, as well as to listen carefully to what others are saying. Unfortunately, this is not always accomplished and a lot of time can be wasted in meetings when communication is poor. Thus, it is important to ensure that all team members communicate effectively.

Following is a closer look at what it means to be an effective communicator and how you can improve your communication skills.

Step 1. Prepare

It is prudent to prepare for all communications, regardless of the number of receivers or the form. This will allow you to ensure you are communicating in the most effective manner and that you have the best chance of achieving the desired outcome. To prepare, you should consider the communication's context, the other participant(s) and the desired outcome.

Consider the questions provided earlier in this chapter as you prepare for a conversation or presentation. Not all of these questions are equally important to every interaction or situation. Think about each of them and answer as many as you can to gain the most insight.

The Basics of Communication

Clarify the objective of the communication. Usually it will be one (or more) of these three:
1. To inform—This type of communication is used to teach or explain something to the listener.
2. To persuade/reach decision—The communicator is seeking to change an individual's beliefs or attitudes on a specific issue or topic. Or, the communicator is informing the listener, providing recommendations and attempting to elicit a decision.
3. To entertain—The communicator is trying to provide enjoyment to the listener.

After you determine the communication's objective, think about how to summarize it clearly and concisely. Use two sentences, at most. For example, "I want to talk to you about…" or " I have called this meeting to get a decision about…"

Next, consider with whom you are communicating:
- What is their familiarity with the topic?
- What is their level of training or education relating to the topic?
- What are their possible biases or objections?
- Are there any cultural considerations?

Are they participating voluntarily, such as someone attending a seminar where you are presenting, or are they assigned or required to participate such as participants in a regulatory agency meeting?

Think about what the other party may be trying to get out of the exchange.

In order to have the most effective conversation, you need to determine their interest. For example, if people are there to listen to you speak about a specific topic, their interest may be educational—learning from you and having their questions answered. If they are regulatory agency employees attending a meeting with you, their interest may be to answer your questions to ensure you prepare a high-quality submission for their review.

Think through all the things you are going to talk about or ask and consider what the possible responses might be so you can ensure clear articulation of your position, prepare additional documentation to support it or to manage any objections to it.

For example, if you are having a meeting with a regulatory agency, one of the most effective preparation techniques you can use is to prepare as many possible responses—both positive and negative—to your questions as you can. Then, consider and prepare your follow-up, including your rationale, references and other supporting information.

What are your desired outcomes?

What end result are you trying to achieve through the communication? If you or the other party(ies) do not know why the conversation is happening, it could lead to a misunderstanding. Some common assumptions that lead to poor (or less than effective) communication:

- We both know what we are talking about.
- We need to agree.
- We know the other person's view.
- We can be brutally honest.
- We need to solve the other person's problem.

To ensure effective communication, try to minimize the number of assumptions that are made within the context of the conversation by ensuring your own understanding and confirming it with the other person(s) during the course of the conversation.

In every communication, you should know precisely what you are trying to achieve. Do you only need to convey information or are you trying to get a decision or elicit an action? If the latter, what exact decision or action do you want? Assuming you cannot get precisely the action, decision or outcome you want, what are the alternatives? Which alternatives can you accept and which do you need to try to negotiate?

Understand the Other Person's Perspective

In addition to knowing your desired outcome, you should determine or try to determine the other party's desired outcome. For example, what is the other party's perspective on the topic? What are their biases or their background and history? How do these factors impact their interpretation of the information you are sharing or the decision or action you are trying to achieve?

To improve understanding, put yourself on the other side of the table or the conversation. What is important to you? What is not important? What do you need or want? You may not know all of these things with certainty, but make an effort to determine what the other party is likely to know already, what they may need to know and how they may understand or believe this knowledge. Be sure to avoid the "curse of knowledge." Once you know something, it is hard to view a topic from

the perspective of those who lack that same knowledge. Furthermore, the stronger your own views and opinions, the less likely you are to look at something from another person's perspective. Even when something seems to be an absolute fact, from another perspective, it might not be true. For example, most of us believe 1+1 = 2 in all cases. However, consider the following:
- In binary, 1+1 = 10
- In mice reproduction, 1+1 = +/-9
- In chewing gum, 1+1 = 1

Depending upon your perspective and the context of the conversation, there may be different truths or more than one acceptable answer.

Step 2. Rehearse

The next step in effective communication is rehearse, rehearse, rehearse. It does not matter whether you are doing a formal presentation to a group, attending a meeting with the regulatory agency or having a conversation with your supervisor. The rehearsal's extent and formality will vary depending upon the party with whom you are going to converse and the objective of the conversation—but rehearsal is critical.

During your rehearsal, you should plan what you are going to say, including a few variations just in case you need to make modifications at the time. Also, rehearse responses to potential objections or counterpoints the other party might make. Finally, practice patience and listening. Here is a methodical format for moving through your rehearsals.

Structure Your Thinking

You have already determined your objective and your desired end result. As you consider the other party's perspective, determine what will be needed to move them to that end result. Do they fully understand the question or issue at hand? What information do they need before they can understand? Are you fully aware of their perspective or would it be beneficial for them to articulate it so you can respond more effectively?

Here is the pattern for a meeting to solve a problem.
- First stage—exploring the problem

    Do not rush! People often want to hurry and solve a problem because they think a solution is the main objective. Staying with a problem can be uncomfortable. However, it is important to discuss the problem fully and dissect it so it can be thoroughly understood

and so you know precisely what needs to be done to resolve it. To bring this portion of a meeting to a close, articulate the actual and precise problem so everyone involved can agree on what it is.
- Second stage—thinking about the solution

  Again, do not rush the solution! Brainstorm without restriction and with an open mind all of the various tasks, actions or changes that might completely or partially solve the problem. After brainstorming some ideas, consider the pros and cons of each option as well as whether some of them could be combined for a synergistic effect. Consider whether they are all practical, whether they can be implemented within the required timeframe, the possible cost in money or people and the likelihood that any or all of the options can solve the problem as articulated and agreed upon in the first stage. Bringing this stage to a close, the appropriate solution(s) should be agreed upon by all parties and responsibilities should be assigned. A follow-up meeting to evaluate the effectiveness of the solution should be scheduled.

Step 3. Logistics

It is important not only to prepare for and rehearse your communication but also to consider logistical and contextual factors that may decrease the communication's effectiveness or the ability to achieve the desired result.

There are three logistical areas to consider: having the conversation at the right time, having enough time for the conversation and ensuring privacy and no distractions. For example, try to ensure that you are having your conversation when the other party(ies) will be at their peak attention time. Make sure they have as much time as you think you will need for the conversation and schedule that time with them so that it is dedicated to you. Finally, make sure you are in a private area where you will not disturb others and they will not overhear confidential information. And, if you are using visual aids, be sure everyone has a copy and that any technical issues have been resolved prior to the discussion.

Chapter Summary

Communication passes information to a receiver. Effective communication passes a precise and accurate message to a receiver and ensures that the receiver understands the message as it was intended. Effective communication is not a skill with which you are born. It is a skill that must be developed over time and refined in such a way that it works for you as a sender and as a receiver. It is important to be self-aware of your communication style and effectiveness and to learn from as many situations as possible. Do not take effective communication for granted. Follow the steps of effective communication—preparation, rehearsal and logistics—to ensure success every time. Recognize potential barriers to effective communication and take action to overcome them so they do distort the message or the desired outcome.

References and Resources
1. Collins English Dictionary, 10th Edition 2009, William Collins Sons & Co. Ltd
2. Communication Education. www.k12.wa.us/curriculuminstruct/communications. Accessed September 2011.
3. Davis K. The McGraw-Hill 36-Hour Course in Business Writing & Communication, 2nd edition. McGraw-Hill. 2010.
4. Newkirk, D. and Crainer, S. Management Lessons from Modern Wars. http://www.strategy-business.com/article/03312?gko=886ae. Accessed September 2011.

Communication and Negotiation

Chapter 1 Quiz *(Answers on page 120)*

1. True or False. Knowing the message you want to convey to someone is 90% of communication. The result or outcome of the communication is up to the receiver of the communication and cannot be determined or influenced by you as the sender.
2. Which of the following statements is TRUE?
   a. Emotional state affects what a person hears and how he communicates.
   b. Everyone hears 100% of what is said; they just choose not to listen to it.
   c. People will not suffer from hearing a fraction of what is said.
   d. It is most important to actively listen during one-on-one communications; however, team meetings will have minutes, so it is not important to actively listen.
3. True or False. A disadvantage of oral communication is that it requires the attentiveness and active participation of the audience to be effective.
4. Name three barriers to effective communication.
5. Which of the following is NOT true about the "first stage of thinking"?
   a. It is a thorough exploration of the problem.
   b. It should end with an articulate, precise problem statement agree by the group.
   c. It can make people uncomfortable.
   d. It should be done as quickly as possible.

Chapter 2
Effective Communication in Practice

Introduction
As shown in the communication models in the previous chapter, communication is a process beginning with a sender who encodes a message and passes it through some medium to a receiver, who decodes the message. If any kind of disturbance blocks or interferes with any step of the communication process, the message may be misunderstood or destroyed. Disturbances in the communication process leave you facing severe problems. It is therefore critical that these barriers be identified and steps taken to eliminate them.

This chapter will review some barriers to effective communication and provide tools to overcome them.

Effective skills can distinguish a superior from an average communicator and result in better relationships, better teamwork and greater understanding.

Chapter Objectives
- Explore the barriers to effective communication.
- Discuss overcoming the barriers.
- Discuss the concepts, skills and practical application of active listening.
- Identify techniques for providing feedback.
- Explain principles and skills for effective teamwork and meetings.

Barriers to Effective Communication
Nothing is so simple that it cannot be misunderstood.
— *Freeman Teague, Jr.*

Anything that prevents understanding of the message is a barrier to communication. There are several barriers in an organization that affect the flow of communication and can make it ineffective.[1] Some of them are discussed below.

Communication and Negotiation

Noise or Environmental Distractions

Noise, bright or poor lighting, distracting clothing, uncomfortable seating or any other stimulus can cause a distraction that may impede communication. Both the sender and receiver must be able to concentrate on the messages being sent to one another. If either person is distracted, the communication likely will be ineffective.

Perception

Perception is how an individual interprets the world around her, according to preconceived attitudes. Perception affects our ability to listen—consciously or subconsciously. For example, if someone of higher status is speaking, we tend to listen uncritically; if someone of lower status is speaking, we may be inclined to dismiss the person. The way someone speaks can also influence our perception, causing us to believe or dismiss a message; for example, if they have an accent, if they do not articulate clearly, or if they talk too quickly, are not fluent or do not use a familiar vocabulary. In general, people tend to hear messages that are important or relevant to them and reject any message that is different from their beliefs or values.

Stress, Emotional State and Time Pressure

When people are under stress or angry, they do not see things the same way and they do not react the same way as when they are calm. At all times, what we hear, see and believe at a given moment is influenced by our emotional state and psychological state of mind. Similarly, if the receiver feels the communicator is rushed, stressed or angry, he may interpret the message being sent as bad, while if the sender is relaxed, happy and jovial, he may interpret the message as good or interesting.

Many times, work assignments within an organization need to be completed within a specific time period, such as a regulatory submission or a response to an FDA request for information. Failure to complete the work or make a response within the timeframe will result in adverse consequences. Under time pressure, formal channels of communication become shorter, resulting in messages that are only partially transferred or not fully understood. In these situations, it is important to make time for effective communication.

Message

When delivering the message, sometimes we believe useful information will automatically be sent or that all information sent will be useful and

Effective Communication in Practice

that certain information will already be known or have no value to others. So, the message may not be delivered as clearly or completely as it should be. Distractions for the receiver can occur when we focus on the facts rather than the idea or when we hear words used differently from the way we use them or prefer to hear them used. For example, if someone uses the word "stewardess" instead of "flight attendant," which you may consider politically incorrect, you may focus on the word and not the message.

People are surrounded by information, continuously flowing from many sources. It is essential to gain the attention of the other party and control the information flow or the message can be misinterpreted or forgotten.

Ourselves

Sometimes we can get in our own way during communication. This can occur in a few different ways.

- When we focus on ourselves during the communication rather than on the other person or on trying to understand the message—Causes can include feeling that we are being attacked, leading to defensiveness; feeling that we know more than the other person so the information is not valuable; or considering ourselves the center of the activity.
- When we do not listen but only hear—This can occur when a message is so repetitive that the receiver no longer listens to it. Or, it can occur if the receiver is unfamiliar with the topic that the sender is discussing and thus lacks the necessary knowledge to understand it, or is engaged in completing another task and has not given sufficient attention to understanding the message.
- When we cannot remember—Each person has a different ability and capacity for retaining information. What we remember and how long we remember it are affected by our interests and level of attentiveness.

Culture or Bias

Our culture, beliefs, past experiences and biases may also interfere with effective communication. They can act as filters or lenses that change the meaning of the message, hampering the communication process.

Organizational Issues

The more complex an organization's hierarchy (i.e., the more managerial levels that exist), the greater the chances that communication will be distorted, misunderstood or lost. Without a concerted effort to communicate across all levels, senior leaders may be the only ones who see the overall picture on a given issue, while people at lower levels are limited to knowledge about their own areas.

Communication that is filtered through one of these barriers causes the message to be distorted. However, the barriers can be overcome.

Overcoming Communication Barriers
Noise or Environmental Distractions

Noise is the major communication barrier that must be overcome to ensure there are no distractions and the message can be heard. It is essential to identify the source of noise and eliminate it by closing a door, moving to a new location, banning cell phones, etc.

Perception

To reduce the barrier of perception within an organization, it is important to recruit the right individuals to do the job. Employees should have a good command of written and spoken language and demonstrate an ability to listen actively. In addition, the organization should give all employees training on its goals, objectives, policies and procedures, as well as any other training necessary for the employee to do his or her job as the company expects it to be done. These activities will go a long way toward ensuring that when employees are discussing company business, they are able to view it from similar perspectives.

Stress, Emotional State and Time Pressure

Although a communicator may be feeling a great deal of stress or emotion, it is important not to show these feelings if they will cause the receiver to misinterpret the message. In other words, the displayed emotions and body language should match the message being sent. For example, if the sender of the message is angry, the receiver may automatically think the message is not good.

Message

It is important to use simple, clear words and to avoid the use of ambiguous words and jargon, including acronyms. Prepare the message with consideration of the audience and what they already know so that your message is clear, targeted and succinct. See the following chapters for more information about preparation, understanding your audience and capturing their attention.

It is also important to select the most appropriate medium for the communication. For example, simple messages can be conveyed orally while complex messages should be conveyed in writing for best comprehension and second review.

Ourselves

When engaged in communication, make a special effort to listen actively. Active listening means hearing the message and then ensuring a proper understanding of what is heard by asking questions.

Culture or Bias

Overcoming communication barriers related to culture, beliefs, past experiences and biases is complicated because they are difficult to recognize. If possible, each individual should take responsibility for eliminating her own potential interferences and keeping an open mind about the communication. However, it is not always possible to ensure that each party will accept this responsibility. Therefore, it is up to you to be prepared, both as the sender and as the receiver. As the sender of a message, it is important that you understand your receivers' potential filters (language differences, cultural differences, organizational level) so you can structure your message appropriately and respond to their reactions with understanding, providing greater clarity. As the receiver of a message, it is important to keep an open mind and actively listen (see below) to what the sender is trying to say before reacting.

Organizational Issues

The simpler the organizational structure, the easier it should be to communicate effectively. If the organization is more complex, it is important to understand the hierarchy and how to most effectively communicate within a multi-level structure.

To overcome communication issues, organizations should teach and practice effective listening. Effective listening promotes organizational relationships and encourages innovation.

Two of the barrier-eliminating activities that have an impact across several of the barriers are active listening and feedback. Following is a closer examination of these activities.

Active Listening

Listening is a significant part of the communication process. Communication cannot take place unless and until a message is heard and retained thoroughly and positively by the receiver. Listening is essential in understanding the other party and effectively responding during the process of communication. Listening is not something that happens to us; rather, it is something that we cause to happen. Listening is an active interaction that demands the ability to integrate, understand, analyze and interpret a variety of inputs in order to search for meaning in a discussion. In short, listening is a skill.

We have been taught to read, write and speak, but few of us have been taught to listen. Some people think listening is only hearing; however, it also encompasses understanding and remembering. Without the ability to understand and remember what is said, the words would be meaningless.

Hearing and listening are not the same things. Hearing is the act of perceiving sound and is involuntary and passive. Listening is a selective activity that involves both receiving the sound and interpreting it. In other words, listening involves decoding the sound or the message into understanding. Listening must be an active process that involves both the body and the mind. Listening requires intentional effort, concentration and interest.

"There is nothing so annoying as to have two people talking when you're busy interrupting." — *Mark Twain, American author*

Exercise 2.1 Listening Skills

Answer the following questions, true or false. (Refer to the answers on page 120 to see how you did.)

1. Listening is an effortless activity.
2. Listening to a message is the same thing as hearing the message.
3. Listening takes at least as much effort and energy as speaking.
4. Listening effectively gives you an advantage in the communication process.
5. It is okay to interrupt during a meeting if I have a really good point.

Effective Communication in Practice

Listening is fast-paced. People can listen and pay attention to words spoken at a rate of 600 to 800 per minute. However, most people speak at only 100 to 175 words per minute. This discrepancy can easily allow the listener's mind to wander to other thoughts or to begin preparing counter discussion points while the speaker is still talking. Active listening, on the other hand, allows listeners to use this speed to further understanding of the speaker. They can consider each word and ensure they understand its meaning so they can fully understand the message, or can ask questions for clarification. Active listening takes as much, if not more, effort and energy as speaking; but, it is worth the effort because it gives you an advantage in communication and can boost your performance. Here are a few guidelines to follow to become an effective active listener:

- In every communication, spend more time listening than talking.
- Be aware of your biases and try to maintain an open mind to the speaker's message.
- Do not become preoccupied with your thoughts or daydreams.
- If more than two people are involved in the communication, allow everyone to speak.
- Do not plan your responses while the speaker is talking; focus on understanding the message and then respond.
- Do not interrupt the speaker or finish his or her sentences.
- Remain calm and open to the message. Do not become angry or close your mind to the message. This will render the communication ineffective.
- Ask clarifying questions and provide feedback to the speaker (see below).
- Take notes on important points during the communication.
- Rephrase or summarize the speaker's message back to him to ensure that you have heard it correctly.

Active listening makes communication more effective. It also encourages better understanding and a positive, professional attitude. Within an organization, it can also lead to better decision making. Effective listening is directly related to our ability to work as a team.

"We listen at about an efficiency rate of 25 percent maximum, and we remember only about 50 percent of what is delivered during a ten minute speech/lecture/communication." (www.managementstudyguide.com)

Feedback

"When you know something, say what you know. When you don't know something, say that you don't know. That is knowledge."

— *Kung Fu Tzu (Confuscius)*

After listening to a message, the receiver typically responds. This response is called feedback. Giving feedback lets the speaker know that the listener understands the message, agrees or disagrees with it, or does not understand and requires clarification. Feedback may be verbal or nonverbal. For example, a listener may nod his head or smile or may sigh or furrow his brow. Responding to email and asking questions are also forms of feedback.

Speakers should use feedback to clarify the message and to help the listener better understand the message so that he or she may respond appropriately.

Effective Communication

Now that we have examined barriers to effective communication, we will look at factors that make communication effective. According to the *Management Study Guide*, the elements of communication are best described as seven Cs.[2]

Completeness

To be effective, a communication must be complete. This means that it must contain all the information needed by the listener to understand the message and provide an adequate response. To ensure that the message is complete, the sender must learn who the receiver or audience is, what they know already and what they need to know in order to respond. Chapters 3 and 4 provide more information about knowing your audience and preparing your message.

Conciseness

Conciseness means using as few words as possible to convey the necessary information. Concise messages are more appealing and comprehensible to a listener.

"I didn't have time to write a short letter, so I wrote a long one instead."

— *Mark Twain, American author*

Consideration

Consideration involves an understanding of the audience, including viewpoint, background, knowledge and biases, so the message can be developed in a way that makes it easy to receive and understand. Show interest in the audience by observing them and looking for feedback from them as the message is being conveyed. The feedback may be nonverbal, such as confused looks, or you may ask questions to ensure they are following the message.

Clarity

Clarity is about using precise words to create a complete and focused message that will not be misunderstood. A clear message will provide all of the details needed for understanding and appropriate action or response, but will not be cluttered with extraneous thoughts or try to achieve too much. Thoughts and ideas should be expressed as clearly as possible.

Concreteness

To be concrete means that the message contains facts and supporting information so it is not misinterpreted. A concrete message also strengthens the receiver's confidence in its worth and validity.

Courtesy

The sender of the message should be courteous and respectful to the receiver by considering the receiver's viewpoint and not being judgmental or biased in the way the message is delivered (refer to Chapter 6 for additional information).

Correctness

Correct communications should be edited and reviewed to ensure they contain no spelling or grammatical errors. Facts and references should be checked for accuracy. Correctness helps ensure the communication will have a positive impact on the receiver.

Communicating effectively is an art that must be practiced. Communicating effectively at work will lead to better output and more success in achieving the organization's goals.

Effective Communication at Work

Following is a summary of how communication can be improved at work:

- Prepare for all communications
    - Be clear about your ideas in your own mind before communicating to others.
    - Put your thoughts and ideas into the appropriate words to make the message clear and concise.
    - Understand who the audience is and consider their viewpoints and what is important to them. Make the discussion relevant to them.
    - Organize meetings with an agenda.
    - Research the topic on which you will speak.
- Avoid distractions
    - Do not conduct a meeting or seminar in a noisy place.
    - Do not discuss private matters that might cause embarrassment in public areas.
    - Do not multi-task when you when you are involved in communication (e.g., responding to email, texting, answering the phone).
- Be an active effective listener and help others do the same
    - Do not attend meetings empty-handed; always bring a notepad and pen to take notes.
    - As the speaker, use white boards or similar aids to increase understanding.
    - As a receiver, provide feedback to speakers and consider feedback from other listeners.
    - Let everyone at a meeting have an opportunity to speak; engage them.
    - Review decisions and action items after a meeting.

Communication Flows in an Organization

In any organization, effective communication is critical. Poor communication can lead to distrustful and disgruntled team members, missed deadlines and higher attrition rates. Good communications can build trust and strengthen teamwork.

In an organization, communication flow occurs in a number of directions, as described below:

Downward

Downward communication flows from a higher level to a lower level. This communication flow is used by managers to give job instructions to employees, provide employees with the oganization's vision and objectives, give feedback on employee performance and inform employees about their job responsibilities and management's expectations. When communicating downward, consider the employees' concerns and what they need to take away from the communication. For example, if there are going to be budget cuts, employees may need reassurance that their jobs will not be lost or that they will still be supported in completion of their objectives. Note that they will generally be interested in the big picture, to see how they individually fit in and how their specific tasks and activities relate to overall strategy. If goals, objectives or work instructions are being communicated, sufficient details should be provided to enable employees to carry out their jobs. The amount of detail will vary depending upon the employee's experience level and familiarity with the specific job task.

Upward

Upward flow of communication is from a lower level to a higher level. It can consist of feedback on how well the organization is functioning, the problems faced by the employees and whether employees have understood messages received through downward communication. When communicating upward, managers' concerns should be taken into consideration, as well as what they need to know. For example, if a decision is needed before work can continue, what are the options, the pros and cons of each, the cost or time impact and long-term implications that need to be considered to allow management to make the decision? Note that managers generally will not be interested in the details of how the work is being done or how the decision will be implemented beyond the impact on the company and its resources and the long-term consequences.

Lateral

Lateral communication occurs among employees (peers) at the same level within the organization. Peer-to-peer communication allows team members to coordinate tasks and solve problems. When delivering communication laterally, consider your peers' concerns and what information they need. For example, an update on the timing of a deliverable from your department that will impact the work they are doing or a work product different from what they expect, is the type of information of concern to them. In general, peers need to know how an event, change or initiative will impact them and their work so that they can determine whether adjustments or new approaches are needed.

Communication and Negotiation

Diagonal

Diagonal communication occurs among workgroups at all levels. When communicating diagonally, take your managers', peers' or subordinates' concerns into consideration and what they need to know. Follow the same principles described in each of the above flows. If you are speaking to a mixed group of several levels, you will need to work in some of the principles from each of the above flows. It is important to find the right balance for the audience. For example, if you are sharing information about your department's impact on several departments within the company, you will want to include some details about the work so people are familiar with what you do. You will want to describe how your department fits into the company's big picture and any specific projects, and how it relates to the other departments—both how their work impacts you and how your work impacts them. And, finally, you will want to convey any relationship issues or ideas for improving efficiency and collaboration.

External

External communication occurs outside the organization with suppliers, vendors, partners, etc. When communicating externally, depending upon with whom you are speaking, you should follow the same principles as described in each of the above flows. Keep in mind that external people will not be familiar with your company's internal workings and priorities unless you share that with them—which you should do if it impacts their activities. You should also remember that the external audience will need to follow their own organizational priorities, objectives and requirements and that may impact your communication or workflows.

Today, teams do much of the work in organizations. And, much of this work gets done when the teams assemble—usually in a meeting. Meetings are important communication drivers within the organization.

Teamwork and Meetings

City Year, a Boston-based, nationwide, nonprofit service organization, has an interesting policy for all its meetings: City Year uses a ground rule called NOSTUESO to keep wordy employees from monopolizing discussions and to ensure that all voices are heard. NOSTUESO is an acronym for "No One Speaks Twice Until Everybody Speaks Once." (www.inc.com)

They help ensure understanding of and buy-in to the organization's goals.

Teamwork

There are some tasks that cannot be accomplished alone. Individuals need to come together as a group and discuss things among themselves and sometimes work together as a team toward the realization of a common goal. A group that is assembled for any purpose is not necessarily a team. A group can have individuals with varied interests, attitudes and thought processes. It is not necessary that the group members have a common objective or goal to achieve.

A team should be formed when the task is more complicated. Ideally a team should consist of seven to 10 members. Having too many members can lead to confusion and misunderstandings in communication. Team members are expected to contribute equally to get the task completed efficiently and effectively. A well-functioning team can accomplish substantial feats.

In a well-functioning team, the members of the team communicate with one another to ensure they are all working in unison toward their common goal and that when they have problems, they are being supported and making adjustments to their work plan. Effective communication forms the cornerstone to ensure team members remain focused and challenge one another without resorting to arguing and deterioration of relationships.

Team Development

Teams develop and mature over a period of time as interdependence and trust grow among the members. There are four stages of team development: forming, storming, norming and performing.[3]

"Coming together is a beginning. Keeping together is progress. Working together is success."   — *Henry Ford*

Stage 1: Forming

During this stage, group members tend to be formal with each other. They will not yet have a clear understanding of their objectives. And, they may not be familiar with the other members of the group and their functions or capabilities.

This is the time when the team needs to prepare or be given its goals. And, more importantly, each individual must personally accept and buy into those goals. For example, management gives the team the goal of preparing an Investigational New Drug (IND) application and filing it with FDA within the next 90 days so clinical studies can begin. The team must establish the actions necessary to accomplish this, and then each individual member must agree to deliver his or her portion of the work so the goal can be met. This process will give clarity to the objective and the individual contributions, as well as establishing the commitment to the goal.

During this process, team members will also be learning about one another and figuring out how to best work together. Communication is important to ensure that relationships are building among the members. Having regular team meetings and talking through objectives, processes and tactics will help advance communication during this stage.

Stage 2: Storming

During this stage, team members are eager to get started on meeting the objective, especially if there is already time pressure. As the tasks begin, conflict may arise as people bring different ideas about how to accomplish the goals. Differences rather than similarities will be accentuated as team members begin showing their individual styles. They will get impatient and they will try to probe one another's areas, which can lead to irritation and frustration, and even to some members' dropping out mentally or physically. As tensions increase, communication is even more important. Conflicts should be discussed and resolved and new boundaries and expectations set. Conflicts that relate to information, documents or tactics that will impact more than two members of the team are best handled within the group setting so each team member who has an interest in the outcome can voice his or her opinion on the topic prior to a decision being made. Conflicts of a more personal nature, or those with an outcome that impacts only two team members, may be most appropriately discussed and resolved in a one-on-one setting with outcomes reported back to the team as appropriate.

Stage 3: Norming

Norming is the stage of team development where the team finds its "normal" state of being. Conflicts from the Storming stage find resolution. Team members begin to recognize that they have similarities to their peers and that they are all in this together. There is greater involvement of team members and more a feeling of "we." The team members are also likely to become more social and relaxed with one another. They may even forget their focus in favor of having a good time and need to be reminded to stay on goal.

Communication in team meetings and through one-on-one interactions during this stage is critical to ensure the members continue to be focused on the same objective, maintain good relationships, resolve conflicts quickly, are brainstorming ideas and staying creative, and are listening to one another so they can reach solutions to team problems.

Stage 4: Performing

During this stage, the team is mature. The members are trained, competent and able to do their own problem solving. The members understand their roles and responsibilities and are self-motivated. The team is able to produce results and performs well.

Communication at this stage remains important, but should be easier among team members who trust one another and have learned to communicate well. During this stage, team members may also have developed their own code language or communication shortcuts that allow them to effectively communicate with one another in a relaxed, comfortable way.

As you can see, team members do not start performing at the very beginning; they need time. It is possible that not all team members will perform equally or that some will not get along well with all of their teammates. When individuals find it difficult to adjust to one another, their performance suffers and ultimately, the whole team suffers. Team management activities (described below) ensure all team members work together toward the common goal.

Consider the following two scenarios:

Scenario 1:

Antoinette worked in a leading organization and managed a team of five skilled team members who reported directly to her. Antoinette made sure she interacted with her team members daily. She would make casual conversation, inquire about their weekend and their families, and was always available if they had questions or problems. The team members were encouraged to stop by her office with their issues or send her an email. They were also encouraged to bring up issues in an open forum during meetings. The team members worked comfortably with one another and sometimes had dinner outside the office. Antoinette's team members were sometimes seen working together late in the office or on weekends to ensure they would meet their targets on time.

Scenario 2:

Claus worked in a leading organization and managed a team of five skilled team members who reported directly to him. He always maintained a professional distance from them, seeing them only in meetings they attended together and conversing with them only to pass along work instructions if needed. He never missed an opportunity to criticize the work of one of his team members if required. No employee was allowed to enter Claus' office without a prior appointment. His team hated working in the office, preferring to work from home just to avoid Claus. The team members worked individually; none was ever willing to help another. Claus' team never achieved their targets within the allotted timeframe.

Which of these teams would you rather be on?

You probably responded that you would rather be on Antoinette's team. What is so special about that team? Antoinette did not do anything special. She just reassured her team members that she was there to listen and they could feel comfortable bringing up their issues. Claus also did nothing special. He did not interact with his team unless necessary and expected them to complete their jobs as instructed. If someone had an issue, he expected them to know how to handle it. So, what is so special about Antoinette's team? Communication. As you can see in these examples, communication—even in its simplest form—can go a long way to make a team comfortable or not, trusting or not and successful or not.

Team Management

Team management refers to the various activities that bind a team together to achieve the set targets. While team management encompasses a number of activities to ensure that team members remain focused on the team's goals, one of the primary elements is continued effective communication in all directions, internal and external to the team.

As demonstrated in the above scenarios, communication plays a very important role in team building and extracting the best out of the team members. Effective and open communication improves relationships among team members and reduces the chance of conflicts among them.

It is important to note that relying solely on oral or spoken communication can sometimes create misunderstanding or confusion and may not be recalled in adequate detail in the future. Therefore, it is important to prepare written communication about important topics for better clarity and transparency. This written communication may be in the form of meeting minutes, email, memos, etc. (see Chapter 4 for additional information about written communication).

A smoothly operating team relies on effective communication among its members. They must speak clearly and concisely so everyone understands what they are saying. They must also be willing to listen and learn from one another. If workers are not cooperating as a team, nothing can be accomplished. So, it is a good idea to set some ground rules for effective communication within the team. Some examples are:

- First <u>understand</u>, and then <u>be understood.</u>
- Be an active listener (refer to above section).
- Be clear and concise. This will save time as well as promote better understanding among the team members.
- Transparency must be maintained within the team. Team members should be encouraged to raise any topic or issue that is relevant to the team.
- Discussion among team members should be encouraged. All team members should have an opportunity to speak.
- Disagreements among team members should be discussed openly and respectfully.
- Avoid negativity within the team.
- Never try to impose your ideas on any member.
- Before implementing any new idea, it must be discussed with the team in an open forum. It is advisable to not discuss ideas with team members separately and individually because the other members may feel left out and reluctant to accept the idea or to continue to perform and contribute to the team.
- Meetings are fundamental to the work of teams. Therefore, when meeting as a team, effective communication is important to ensure time is not wasted and the team continues to advance toward its goals and objectives. When meeting as a team, members should practice the Five Commandments of team meeting behavior:

1. **Do not interrupt.**
   How many times have you been interrupted when you were speaking?

If you are like most people, someone started interrupting you at a young age. Perhaps it was one of your parents or a friend. As you got older, you might have been interrupted by a professor at college or by a co-worker on the job. Most people who interrupt do not mean to be rude. In fact, they may not consciously realize they are interrupting the speaker. They are so eager to express their opinions they simply cannot wait for the speaker to finish. Perhaps you are the type of person who interrupts others frequently for this very reason.

Unfortunately, teams do not operate well when members interrupt one another. Everyone deserves an equal chance to be heard. If an employee is cut off in mid-sentence or is interrupted while presenting an important idea, he or she is likely to feel unappreciated or disrespected. The person may even begin to feel resentful toward the team or the individual who interrupts him—especially if it happens repeatedly. Teams cannot function efficiently if resentment builds up among members. When members do not get along, a team quickly loses its spirit of teamwork and will likely have less desire to win. Interrupting might also prevent an employee from saying something that could be vital to a project's success. In the best-functioning teams, every member has a chance to contribute and is encouraged to do so.

2. Do not jump to conclusions.

Since people can process information much more quickly than they can speak, it is easy to stop paying attention to the speaker and begin thinking about something else. Then, when you miss important things that were said while you were not listening, you may make erroneous assumptions or jump to the wrong conclusion to fill in the gaps.

3. Do not judge the messenger.

Sometimes we let our opinions of a speaker or a speaker's mannerisms prevent us from listening carefully to what is being said. Consider the following example: a manager who is used to dealing with people who speak quickly, and also likes to talk pretty quickly herself, admits that whenever she has to listen to someone who speaks slowly, she begins to get impatient and even stops listening or interrupts with her response. "Why can they not just get to the point?" she has said.

Whether we like to admit it or not, each of us has certain biases that can get in the way of effective listening. It is important to evaluate people and their messages on their own merits. Some common biases can be based on the following:

How the speaker sounds

If a person has an unfamiliar accent, you may find yourself judging what is said without really listening. Perhaps this individual comes from a different region of the country or a different part of the world. Perhaps he or she speaks more quickly or slowly than you.

How the speaker looks

The first thing you notice about people is their appearance. What kind of clothes are they wearing? How much jewelry? It is easy to let someone's appearance—especially someone who looks different from you—stand in the way of effective communication. Donald Walton points out that judging people based on appearance is one of the emotional obstacles that can prevent you from giving rational consideration to what someone is saying. Walton urges people to concentrate on what is being said rather than who is saying it.[4] He says that the following are questions you should consider instead of focusing on appearances: Is it true? Does it sound right to me? Is it contrary to or in line with the facts that I have previously heard?

The speaker's age

Ageism can be a barrier to effective communication. If you are younger and a person has gray hair, you may assume that he cannot relate to you. Likewise, adults may feel that teenagers or young adults are too inexperienced to teach them anything. This is another example of an emotional generalization that can prevent effective listening.

Put yourself in the speaker's place

Good listeners have the ability to empathize with a speaker. They try to read the speaker's body language to discern the rest of the message and respond accordingly. Empathetic listeners can provide verbal or nonverbal encouragement, which can enable the speaker to communicate more easily and effectively. For example, the speaker might appear tense, which could indicate nervousness. If the speaker's tone of voice is emotional or tentative, it may indicate that she is upset. The listener might encourage the speaker by saying, "It looks like there is something you would like to talk about." Listeners can also communicate their interest and encouragement by nodding their heads, smiling or making eye contact.

Remember, only 7% of our message comes through the words we use; 38% comes through our tone of voice and 55% comes through our body language.[5]

4. Do not be self-centered.
Listen to what other team members have to say. Do not monopolize the discussion.

5. Do not tune out.
On the job, we may be required to sit through many meetings and training sessions. If we allow ourselves to get bored and distracted, chances are we will not listen very carefully to what is being said. So, how do you beat boredom and keep focused on the message being conveyed?

One way is to look for something of value in what the speaker is saying—something that can benefit you. For example, suppose you have just gone to work at a new company and you are sitting through a two-day orientation program. At this orientation, speakers from various departments talk about their operations and how they contribute to the company's success. These programs can be long and tedious—if you approach them that way. Or, they can give you a chance to find out where you might eventually like to work within the organization. Perhaps one department sounds particularly interesting, with plenty of opportunity for growth. This might be the place on which to set your sights.

Another way to stay focused during a long presentation is to take notes. You do not have to worry about all the details; just listen for the main ideas and write them down. This will help you concentrate on the main points and avoid becoming distracted. Some presentations are followed by question-and-answer sessions. It is often a good idea to formulate your own questions while listening to the speaker. This is another way to concentrate on what he or she is saying, avoid boredom and focus your attention on the main ideas. Good questions will provide you with additional information. Asking questions also gives you a way to stand out from your peers and show that you are listening carefully.

Teams should also follow the important steps for effective meetings that are discussed below.

Meetings
"Whoever invented the meeting must have had Hollywood in mind. I

think they should consider giving Oscars for meetings: Best Meeting of the Year, Best Supporting Meeting, Best Meeting Based on Material from Another Meeting." — *William Goldman, American author*

Managers and other workers spend one-fourth of their week in meetings. Since meetings are such a critical part of business, it is important to understand how to make these interactions as effective as possible and not waste time.

According to consultants Roger Mosvick and Robert Nelson, authors of *We've Got to Start Meeting Like This! A Guide to Successful Meeting Management,* the number of business meetings is growing. But that does not mean that people are getting more work done. In fact, they report that "over 50 percent of the productivity of the billions of meeting hours is wasted." This tremendous waste of time is attributed to poor meeting preparation and lack of training in how to conduct meetings effectively. A well-run meeting combines writing, speaking and listening skills. Whether you are leading a meeting or participating in one, you need to communicate clearly and effectively.

Successful meetings are productive, well organized and creative. For a meeting to be successful and effective, it must be well planned. In addition to identifying the time and place, it is important to define the objective of the meeting and to create an agenda that will achieve that objective. The objective and the agenda will determine who the participants should be. If it is expected that any of the participants prepare in advance of the meeting, they should be informed of these expectations.

Meetings should begin on time and should remain focused on the agenda. Attendees should be instructed to keep distractions minimized, e.g., no cell phone calls. At the end of the meeting, give a brief summary of any decisions and action items. Prepare meeting minutes that provide the decisions and action items minimally.

Effective communication in a group requires participation from all attendees. It is important for attendees to be prepared to discuss the topic of the meeting and to represent the area that they are intended to cover.

Communication within a meeting requires the use of the above skills and techniques for effective communication. Stay calm and composed and do not react emotionally in the meeting.

The steps to prepare for an effective meeting include planning an agenda and having the right people; conducting the meeting to ensure that you get the most out of it; and then following up after the meeting. Following is a look at each of these steps for an effective meeting in more detail.

Planning an Agenda

In a large office, a group of managers sit around discussing the annual company outing. They talk and talk. They trade stories about past company outings. Then they complain to each other about problems in their departments. Finally, they start to wonder whether there should be an outing at all this year. After three hours, nothing is accomplished, even though all the outing arrangements were supposed to be finalized by the end of the week.

Meetings can become long-winded dialogues where nothing is accomplished. One way to avoid this problem is to carefully structure the meeting. That structure is called an agenda. As authors Richard Chang and Kevin Kehoe explain, "Just as the developer works from a blueprint and shares it with other people working on the building, a meeting should have a 'blueprint.' The blueprint or agenda provides everyone with a picture of what the meeting will look like."[6]

The most critical element of any meeting agenda is the objective, which addresses the purpose of the meeting. If you are writing a memo or report, your first job is to determine its purpose and describe it in the introduction. Similarly, if you are leading a meeting, one of your responsibilities is to establish its objectives, making sure they are described in the agenda.

When developing an agenda, write a sentence for each objective. Short summary sentences tell the participants what you want to cover in the meeting and what you hope to accomplish—informing, deciding, brainstorming, etc. This way you can avoid having a meeting that goes onto a tangent in the wrong direction.

Your next step is to set a date, time and place for the meeting and prepare an agenda. Define your objective and the names of the participants as well as any preparation that is required from participants in advance of the meeting.

People and Preparation

In a study of executives conducted by the Wharton Center for Applied Research at the University of Pennsylvania, a majority reported that there are too many people participating in meetings. Many meetings include people who do not need to be present and do not make meaningful contributions. Therefore, only invite people who absolutely have to attend.

And, assign them roles at the meeting.

Conducting the Meeting

The meeting leader's role is to make sure the meeting follows the agenda. A meeting that stays on track is less likely to waste time. The leader is also responsible for concluding the meeting by reviewing any decisions and/or actions that were agreed upon during the meeting. This final review ensures that everyone understands the decisions and actions coming out of the meeting or can ask for clarification so the group will have accomplished a meaningful goal.

Meeting Follow-up

Most of what is said during a meeting will be forgotten or will be remembered differently by each participant. Therefore, it is important to prepare minutes of the meeting and send them to each participant. Minutes of the meeting may be as simple as recording decisions and action items or as complex as including details on all topics discussed.

Virtual Meetings

Virtual meetings, in which one or more individuals participate via the Internet or telephone, are more prevalent and necessary in the business world today. While web-based collaboration and teleconferencing save money and time, they can also present challenges to participants. For example, it may be difficult to set up a meeting time that works for attendees in New York, Tokyo and Berlin. Connectivity issues may also cause the meeting to be less effective. Here are a few tips that will help you communicate successfully during Internet and telephone meetings.

- Pay attention—Resist the urge to let your focus wander when not actively participating.
- Clarify confusing or complex conversations—The technology for virtual meetings has improved greatly, but it is still no substitute for face-to-face meetings. If a participant says something you do not understand or refers to a document that you cannot view, speak up so you can understand what is being discussed.
- Get everyone online—If it is necessary to view a document or slide presentation during the meeting, make sure all parties receive the document in advance or they are all online for the meeting. Also, if the presentation will be live, complete a test run of how the software loads, how slides are viewed by participants,

whether there is a lag in changing slides and so on. This will help reduce the need for pauses in the discussion to summarize what is in the document or presentation or to clarify issues. Follow up with participants to find out how their virtual experience was and what might be done differently the next time.

Chapter Summary

Important characteristics of effective communicators are excellent listening skills and the ability to present information in both formal and informal settings. Effective communicators also maximize the benefits of group communication in a meeting and minimize the amount of time wasted. This can be accomplished by using an agenda and good meeting management.

While it may be easy to recall the various characteristics of active listening, including resisting distraction, using your thought speed, holding your response, remembering to identify the purpose and main point and not interrupting, the challenge truly lies in implementing these seemingly simple techniques. They are challenging because they do not occur automatically. Active listening requires active strategies. It is also not easy, since the many demands on our attention make it difficult to concentrate on what is being communicated.

Chapter 2 Quiz (*Answers on page 121*)
1. True or False. Work communications can be improved if you are an effective listener, avoid distractions, and prepare for all of your communications.
2. The most critical element of any meeting agenda is:
   a. Start time
   b. Attendees
   c. Objective
   d. Location
3. True or False. You can improve your active listening skills by asking yourself the following questions:
   - Do I really know what the other person is talking about?
   - Could I repeat what I heard?
   - Can I remember what I heard?
4. Which of the following is not one of the seven Cs of communication?
   a. Clarity
   b. Comprehensive
   c. Conciseness
   d. Correctness
5. Communicating with your boss is an example of which type of communication flow?
   a. Downward
   b. Lateral
   c. Diagonal
   d. Upward

References
1. Communication Barriers—Reasons for Communication Breakdown. www.managementstudyguide.com/communication_barriers.htm (accessed 14 September 2011).
2. Seven C's of Effective Communication. www.managementstudyguide.com/seven-cs-of-effective-communication.htm (accessed 14 September 2011).
3. Tuckman B. "Developmental sequence in small groups." *Psychological Bulletin*, 1974.
4. Walton D. *Are You Communicating? You Can't Manage Without It*. McGraw-Hill Education, 1989.
5. Hymes D. *Foundations in Sociolinguistics: An Ethnographic Approach (Conduct and Communication)*. Univ. of Pennsylvania Press. 1974.
6. Chang R and Kehoe K. *Meetings That Work! A Practical Guide to Shorter and More Productive Meetings*. John Wiley & Sons, 1999.

Communication and Negotiation

Additional Resources

Wolvin AD, ed. *Listening and Human Communication in the 21st Century*. John Wiley & Sons, 2009.

Davis K. *The McGraw-Hill 36-hour Business Course: Business Writing and Communication*. McGraw-Hill, 2010.

Chapter 3

Oral and Behavioral Communication

Introduction

People generally communicate in three ways:
1. Oral (spoken)
2. Behavioral (nonverbal) and
3. Visual, including writing

Oral communication refers to spoken words. Oral communication includes one-on-one and group discussions and presentations.

Oral communication typically relies on visual aids and nonverbal elements to deliver or support the meaning of the message. Nonverbal communication refers to conveying a message without using words and includes gestures, "body language," facial expressions and eye contact.

Written communication refers to words on paper or transmitted electronically. Visual communication refers to words, pictures, graphs, charts and other images that are intended to be seen and understood by the receiver of the message. Visual communication includes posted signs and slide presentations. Written communication—words on paper or digital media—is a subset of visual communication.

This chapter and the next will review details specific to each of these methods of communication.

Chapter Objectives

- Understand the oral and behavioral methods of communication.
- Prepare for and give better presentations.
- Effectively use and interpret body language communication.

Oral Communication

Employers surveyed in 2007 by OfficeTeam rated oral communication skills as the second most important soft skill in demand among administrative staff at their companies, whereas the ability to write for business ranked sixth.[1]

Communication and Negotiation

Oral communications may be formal, such as a speech or presentation; semiformal, such as professional discussions in a meeting or with your supervisor or subordinates; or informal, such as those with your friends and family. Oral communication may occur face-to-face or over the phone or Internet (VoIP). In face-to-face communication, body language and voice tonality play a significant role and may have a greater impact on the listener than the content of the spoken words. Consider the following example.

You are in a project team meeting and are asked by the team leader to express your opinion on a topic. When you begin speaking, you make eye contact with various people around the table and you speak with confidence. The person sitting across from you arches an eyebrow skeptically while listening to you speak. Seconds later, the same person crosses his arms over his chest, narrows his eyes, creases his forehead and tilts his head down.

Do you think that he is in agreement or disagreement with what you are saying? He does not need to say a single word to give you a certain impression about what he is thinking. It may not always be correct, but it is still an impression. More will be covered about nonverbal communication later in the chapter.

Becoming a better communicator in general will improve your ability to participate effectively in formal, semiformal and informal settings.

Semiformal Oral Communication

Semiformal settings for communication at work primarily include one-on-one or group meetings and discussions.

Whenever possible, you should do as much as you can to prepare for the meeting in advance. You can review the meeting agenda, conduct research, make notes about key points that you need to cover on a specific topic or write down clarifying questions that must be answered before you will be able to progress your work further. If no meeting agenda is available, you should ask the meeting organizer what topics will be discussed during the meeting. If you are controlling the meeting, you should prepare an agenda or at a minimum, define the meeting objective and share it with the attendees. Refer to Chapter 2 for more information on general meeting preparation.

The keys to effective speaking are energy and confidence. When you begin speaking during a meeting, it is important that you are clear in your thoughts so you can communicate them to the other attendees in an organized manner. You should also be familiar with the topic so you are confident when you speak and when you are questioned or challenged on the topic. Speaking with energy can keep people involved and prevent them from becoming distracted or even falling asleep! You can add energy with your voice by emphasizing certain words or ideas to indicate their importance. By changing your speaking volume, you can also add variety to your presentation.

Gestures are another way to add energy. As you speak, use nonverbal communication to reinforce your message. For example, if you are listing three objectives, use your fingers to indicate the first, second and third points. If you are making a key point, jab the air with your forefinger or fist to drive the point home. If you are asking for support from participants, stretch out your hands to them. Gestures and reinforcing nonverbal communication automatically raise the vocal energy of your talk and better engage the audience. In fact, if you use gestures, it is almost impossible to speak in a monotone. At the same time, be careful not to overuse gestures to the point where they become distractions to the audience.

"Nothing builds rapport faster than eye contact. Building rapport is critical for achieving audience buy-in—and without 100 percent buy-in, it's terribly difficult to inspire an audience to act."
— *Tony Jeary in Inspire Any Audience: Proven Secrets of the Pros for Powerful Presentations*

Making eye contact with your listeners is another way to keep them involved. As you begin a thought, look at one listener. Continue looking at that individual until you complete the thought. Then select another listener and repeat the process. This enables you to establish a dialogue with all participants, which is an effective way to keep them focused on what you are saying.

It can be difficult to know exactly how you come across to others during meetings. Ask meeting attendees you trust to give you feedback on your style, your listening abilities and their recommendations for improvements. You want to target a speaking style that directly influences others and commands their attention. You can practice presenting your ideas or stating your position and record yourself to get an understanding of how you sound to others. You can also try to find a mentor. Ask a

Communication and Negotiation

peer with a good speaking style to help you analyze how you sound and give you tips on how to make improvements. Specifically, listen to your recording and ask for feedback on the following:
- Is my level of enthusiasm and liveliness appropriate for the topic?
- Is the language I use simple enough for others to understand easily?
- Are my tone of voice and inflection consistent with the meaning of my words and the intent of the message?
- Does the pace of speech facilitate understanding?
- Are there nervous tics or word fillers (e.g., "um," "ahh," "like") I need to remove?

In addition to speaking and using appropriate nonverbal communication, it is important to remember that one-on-one and group meetings are forms of two-way communication. This means you also need to observe the audience and get feedback from them so you can ensure they understand your message. If anyone appears confused or unclear, you must clarify the message. This can include rephrasing the message, providing an example or simply asking the audience if they have any questions or require clarification on your points.

Two-way communication also means you need to be an active and effective listener. Regardless of whether you are a speaker in the meeting, you need to be a listener. Active and effective listeners try to understand what the speaker is saying, ask clarifying questions and take note of key points for later reflection.

How do you ask clarifying questions without being offensive to the speaker or without seeming to pass judgment before you have an understanding of the speaker's message? At the most basic level, you ask open-ended questions. This means that the responder cannot answer yes or no. He or she must provide a more substantive response. To ask questions in this manner, use phrases beginning with "what," "how," "describe" or "explain." As an exercise in formulating good questions, review the questions below and determine which are open-ended and will elicit additional meaningful information from the responder and which are closed-ended.

Despite your best efforts, there may be some barriers that disrupt your ability to get through to a difficult subordinate, peer, superior or other person. If you have problems communicating with a particular individual,

Oral and Behavioral Communication

> **Exercise 3.1 Clarifying Questions**
> Which of the following questions are open-ended and which are closed-ended?
> a. Open
> b. Closed
>
> 1. Do you have references to back up your facts and assumptions?
> 2. What are the assumptions you have made in order to reach your conclusions?
> 3. Do you think you would change your conclusions if you changed your assumptions to be [some modification]?
> 4. Are you confident in your facts and your assessment?
> 5. What gives you confidence in your facts and assessment?
> 6. Do you think there is a risk to your proposal?
> 7. What are the risks associated with your proposal?
> 8. Will this proposal fit within the current timeframe and cost assumptions?
> 9. What are the impacts to the timeline and cost?
>
> (*Answers on page 121*)

examine your interaction using the list of potential barriers below:
- Are you failing to understand or appreciate his or her personal motives?
- Are you showing a lack of concern or not giving feedback (see later section)?
- Are you trying to protect your prestige or position while communicating?
- Are you withholding relevant information or telling half-truths?
- Do either of you have a hidden agenda or message?
- Are there distractions, excessive noise or a lack of privacy?
- Are you intimidating or talking down to subordinates?
- Do you distrust the speaker or does he or she distrust you?
- Are you failing to take the time or devote the energy to listen?

Most of the same principles apply to formal oral communication. But, there is some additional preparation and practice you may want to do.

Formal Oral Communication

We are sometimes called upon to deliver information in a formal manner. Your supervisor, a committee, a customer or a fellow employee may request structured delivery of information. Regardless of whether it is a presentation, a description of new procedures to be implemented or a demonstration of the advantages of a system or solution, these formal occasions require delivery of information in a one-way communication style.

A great presenter will capture the attention of the audience, connect with them and entertain them. A poor presenter will bore the audience or leave them confused.

What does it take to be a great speaker? Some might say that you have to be born with "it." Perhaps it is true that some great speakers are born. However, most just make it look easy and they actually do a lot of hard work before they begin to give a formal presentation. They develop their own way of engaging the audience and keeping them engaged throughout the presentation.

"It takes three weeks to prepare a good ad-lib speech."
— *Mark Twain, American author*

While every person needs to individualize the steps and get comfortable with how they will engage the audience in a way that works for them, there are some recommended preparation steps to take before any presentation.

Preparing to Speak

Most importantly, before you speak, you must be clear about the goal of the communication. Are you training people, informing them about a topic, trying to persuade them? And, what are you talking to them about? Who are the audience members and what do they know already? What do they expect to know or what do you think they need to know by the time the presentation is over? What content does it take to bridge that gap? Following is a closer look at each of these steps.

Know the purpose or objective of your presentation.

The first step is to be clear on the purpose of your formal communication. Are you providing new or updated information, teaching a new procedure or orienting a group of new employees? Are you trying to get a group to make a decision or take an action? What results or other outcome will let you know you have been successful? You should be able to articulate your purpose in one to two short sentences.

Know your audience and what they already know.

The first step to ensuring you can engage your audience is to know who the members are. You must know this so you can prepare your presentation for this audience.

Donald Walton, in his book *Are You Communicating?*, advises that "before you start, it's wise to reflect on who your audience will be and what their primary interests are."

Although you cannot always gain specific information about all members of your audience, you should try to understand their educational and cultural backgrounds as well as their likely thought processes. For example, if you are presenting at a professional meeting sponsored by the Regulatory Affairs Professionals Society, your audience is likely to be comprised of individuals who have either scientific or legal backgrounds and are familiar with regulatory terminology. Depending upon the topic of the presentation or its classification level (e.g., beginner) and topic category (e.g., drugs), you may be able to deduce additional useful information about the likely audience, such as their number of years of experience, their specialization in the field and their potential interest in the topic.

Also, ask yourself what perspective or attitude your audience may have toward your topic. Is your topic controversial? Are you taking an unpopular approach? Do you need to persuade the audience?

What should they know at the end of the communication?

After you have gauged the level of the audience and their perspectives, you need to determine what they are likely to care about related to the topic. What motivates them to listen to you and what do they hope to get out of the communication? What do they need to know about the subject in order to be able to put it into practice? How do you think they will prefer to receive this information, e.g., with stories, anecdotes, facts? For example, using statistics to get your point across is only useful if your audience is comfortable with numbers. If you need to persuade your audience, what approach should you use? Generally, it is something that is unexpected about the topic or will make it more important and immediate to them.

For example, suppose you have been asked to give a presentation to a group of college students about the importance of not smoking or quitting smoking. Chances are, they have already heard from the media, their parents, some friends or others that smoking causes health problems up to and including death. It is also likely that they are able to read the 30-point font on the cigarette package that says "Smoking Kills." If they still smoke or are planning to start, it is unlikely that a repeat of these messages will be persuasive. Since they are young and healthy and feel invincible or at least believe they will not have to worry about death for 30 or 40 years, telling them to stop for health benefits or to live longer is a far-off goal and unlikely to be persuasive.

Instead, you should look at their perspective of why they smoke or are considering smoking and find a more immediate reason why they need to quit. Many people become smokers or continue to smoke because it is relaxing and social. Thus, if they were to quit smoking, they would be more stressed, nervous and less social; possibly less accepted by their friends. These are strongly compelling and immediately current reasons to start or continue smoking. A persuasive speaker would need to find strong and immediate counter points that could be just as important. Perhaps you could show statistics on cost, e.g., the average smoker spends more than $3,000 (US) a year on cigarettes (based on 1 pack/day and a cost of $7/pack). This same amount could be used for two or three months' rent or a down payment on a car. Working for the minimum wage in the US, it takes one hour of work for every pack purchased, and so on. Another counter point may be discussing how tar and nicotine stain teeth, showing an example of a non-smoker vs. a smoker.

Understanding what the audience knows and believes and what it likely to be important to them will allow you to frame the message and develop the content that will best resonate.

What content does it take to bridge the gap?

Begin to prepare your presentation or speech by stating the key points that you want to communicate. Generally, try to use no more than five key points so there is enough time to provide some depth to the message. Use these key points to create an outline of the presentation, making brief notes of what you will say about each one. Then, fill in the outline with what you know and what you develop through research.

Continue to keep your audience in mind as you prepare your presentation. Remember, presentations do not have to be long to be

Oral and Behavioral Communication

effective. US President Abraham Lincoln's Gettysburg Address is a perfect example. It is one of the most memorable speeches ever delivered by a US leader, yet it lasted only a few minutes and was a mere 268 words in length. For comparison, that is about the same length as this section.

The best formal communications are concise and compelling. Make sure all the information you present strengthens your purpose and supports your key points. Keep it simple and self-explanatory. Choose your words carefully. Use short sentences and cover only as much information as you need to meet the purpose of your presentation.

Support your message with visual aids including graphs, diagrams and pictures to make the presentation more interesting and give it more impact (read more about visual communication in Chapter 4). Try to include examples from real-life situations to illustrate your points and make them more relevant and practical for the audience.

Rehearse.

Before delivering any presentation, read it aloud once or twice so you can develop confidence with the material. You must be clear with each and every slide, including the overall flow and the segues between slides. If you have time, record a rehearsal with audio or video and critique yourself or ask others to do so. Rehearse in the location where the actual presentation will take place, if you can. This will give you an idea of the room's acoustics and special aspects.

All the above tips will help you prepare a presentation, but the presentation will not be effective unless and until you deliver it effectively. The content of your message and your communication skills go hand-in-hand to create a great presentation. Do not be too self-conscious; just be yourself, practice your presentation, know your material, approach your presentation with confidence and you will never fail.

Delivering the Presentation

Speak comfortable words! — William Shakespeare

There is no magic formula for delivering a good presentation. Be assured that all the great speakers you have seen had to work hard to excel. They probably practiced speaking in front of groups continuously to become so comfortable and make it look effortless. If you want to become a great speaker, just start giving presentations. With every one that you give, you will refine your style and increase your comfort, and become better and better.

Here are a few things you should try to do during the presentation to best engage the audience and communicate your message.

- Always begin your presentation with a warm smile. It actually works! Greet your audience and create a friendly ambience. Start your presentation by introducing yourself as well as your organization, if appropriate. The first impression is a lasting impression and the five minutes of introduction must be very effective and powerful to capture the audience's interest so they are with you until the end. Prepare your introduction and practice it once or twice.

- Go through your slides one by one and explain them confidently. Do not rush through the presentation or read the slides. Make eye contact with the audience; do not speak to your slides or to a podium.

- Do not speak too quickly; pause between ideas so the audience can absorb the material.

- Make sure your nonverbal communication is in alignment with your message. For example, if you are speaking about a decline in the performance of your department, smiling and appearing positive are not the most appropriate nonverbal signals.

- Maintain good posture and do not play with a pen or tie or other object. Do not yawn or chew your nails.

Take the time to make your presentation exciting and impressive. You owe that to the listeners.

Conquering Your Fear of Public Speaking

The ability to deliver an effective talk is an extremely valuable skill. If you want to be a leader in any organization, public speaking is usually essential. You must be able to lead meetings, persuade colleagues, team members and management and communicate with internal and external colleagues. Career counselor Rozeanne Burt explains, "The people who can stand up and give a talk stand out and are set apart from other employees."

A fear of public speaking affects about 75% of us. Speaking anxiety affects about the same percentage of women as men, although men are more apt to seek treatment to address their fear, perhaps due to their prevalence in management and leadership positions.[2] There are several approaches that can be used to conquer these fears.

Enlist the help and support of the audience.

Remember that people in the audience genuinely want you to succeed. They know how hard it is to speak in front of a group and they admire you for being brave enough to do it. They have come to hear you speak and want to know what you have to say. They will understand that you may be nervous or that you may make a few mistakes and they will not hold that against you.

Make eye contact with an individual in the audience who is a friend or acquaintance or seems to be attentive and supportive. As you begin, speak to that individual just as though you were having a one-on-one conversation. This will make your speech seem less intimidating. If you are still nervous, take a deep breath and remind yourself that you do not have to be so serious and try to relax.

Make your stage fright work for you.

Stage fright is setting in if you have:
- dry mouth
- sweaty or cold hands
- rapid pulse
- tight throat
- nervous or upset stomach
- shaky lips, knees or hands

Stage fright or fear requires a lot of energy. Instead of letting your fear undermine your talk, channel this energy in other directions such as using gestures to reinforce the main points of your talk. This will allow you to release the fear's energy and will make your talk more dynamic and interesting to the audience. Communications consultant Richard Southern suggests that you "get your body involved in what you're saying." This will add power to your presentation and keep your audience involved from beginning to end.

Tom Antion, author of the article, "Learn How to Be a Professional Speaker," advises: "Try to think of stage fright in a positive way. Fear is your friend. It makes your reflexes sharper. It heightens your energy, adds a sparkle to your eye and color to your cheeks. When you are nervous about speaking you are more conscious of your posture and breathing. With all those good side effects, you will actually look healthier and more attractive."

Be confident; be prepared.

In his book, *Inspire Any Audience,* Tony Jeary[3] explains that one way to overcome pre-speech jitters is to "know what you're talking about. Thorough preparation equals total confidence." Some speakers try to ad-lib and hope for the best, but they often fall flat on their faces and fail to impress the audience. Gaining confidence from being thoroughly prepared is the key to successful public speaking.

Nonverbal Communication/Body Language

To deliver the full impact of a message, nonverbal communication is important. Nonverbal communication comprises all unspoken messages. According to *The Definitive Book of Body Language,*[4] the oral component of face-to-face communication accounts for less than 35% of the message while 65% is nonverbal. Based on Pease's research, nonverbal communication accounts for 60–80% of the impact made around the negotiating table, and 60 80% of the initial opinion about a new person is formed within the first four minutes of interaction.

Generally, we communicate nonverbally and interpret nonverbal communication intuitively. To be the most effective communicator, however, it is important to consciously observe and interpret nonverbal communication and use it effectively to reinforce your messages.

- Context

  It is important to understand the context of the nonverbal communication because different gestures could mean different things, depending upon the situation. If someone is sitting with his arms and legs crossed tightly and his head hunched down, you might read this posture as being closed off or defensive. But if the person were sitting at a bus stop on a cold winter day, you would be more likely to read the gestures as some who was cold and attempting to get warm.
- Gestures

  To interpret someone's nonverbal gestures, it is important to avoid imbuing a single gesture with meaning but rather to

observe the gestures in total. Therefore, a grouping of at least three gestures should be observed to give a more accurate interpretation.

If you fail to gesture while speaking you may be perceived as boring and stiff. A lively speaking style captures the listener's attention, makes the conversation more interesting and facilitates understanding.

- Agreement
  Nonverbal communication holds about five times the meaning of spoken language. When interpreting nonverbal communication, it is important to see whether there is agreement between the nonverbal communication signals and the spoken word. If the two disagree, most people will believe the nonverbal communication.
- Eye contact
  People who make eye contact open the flow of communication and convey interest, concern, warmth and credibility.
- Facial Expressions
  Smiling is a powerful cue that transmits happiness, friendliness, warmth and liking. Smiling is often contagious and people will react favorably. They will be more comfortable around you and will want to listen more.
- Posture and body orientation
  You communicate numerous messages by the way you talk and move. Standing erect and leaning forward communicate to listeners that you are approachable, receptive and friendly. Speaking with your back turned or looking at the floor or ceiling should be avoided as it communicates disinterest.
- Vocal
  Speaking can signal nonverbal communication when you include such vocal elements as tone, pitch, rhythm, timbre, loudness and inflection. For maximum effectiveness, learn to vary these six elements of your voice. One of the major criticisms of many speakers is that they use a monotone and therefore are perceived as boring and dull.

Giving Feedback

Feedback provides information to the speaker about whether the message is being understood. In addition to watching for cues from the audience to ensure they understand the message, make sure there are opportunities for listeners to provide feedback. Ask listeners whether they understand the message and give them the opportunity to ask questions.

Chapter Summary

When communicating orally, it is important to remember there are two factors to your communication—the oral message, including content, voice tone and confidence, and the nonverbal message, including nonverbal communication, emphasis and behavioral aspects of speaking. The most effective oral communicators learn how to manage all parts of their message (oral as well as nonverbal) so it comes across clearly and effectively to the listener.

Chapter 3 Quiz (Answers on page 121)

1. True or False. Always begin your presentations with a smile.
2. Energy in a presentation helps keeps people involved. Which of the following is not a good way to inject energy?
   a. Energetic speaking
   b. Emphasizing certain words when you speak
   c. Jabbing in the air with your finger to make a point
   d. Speaking in a monotone
3. True or False. The keys to effective communication are confidence and energy.
4. True or False. The oral component of communication accounts for less than 35% of the message.
5. When interpreting gestures in nonverbal communication, how many gestures need to be observed in order to get a more accurate interpretation.
   a. 5
   b. 3
   c. 4
   d. 1

References
1. Fitting In, Standing Out and Building Remarkable Work Teams. www.officeteam.com/fiso.
2. Speech Topics Help, Advice & Ideas. www.speech-topics-help.com/fear-of-public-speaking-statistics.html.
3. Jeary T. *Inspire Any Audience: Proven Secrets of the Pros for Powerful Presentations*, 1998, Trade Life Books.
4. Pease. *The Definitive Book of Body Language*, 2004, Bantam Dell.

Communication and Negotiation

Chapter 4

Written Communication

Introduction

Visual communication refers to words, pictures, graphs, charts and other materials that are intended to be seen and understood by the receiver of the message. Visual communication examples include posted signs and slide presentations. It is considered a one-way form of communication. This means there is no immediate opportunity for the reader to follow up and ask clarifying questions. Therefore, writing and graphics must be as clear, concise and accurate as possible so the reader will receive the intended message. Visual communication has the benefit of enduring—it can be retained, referenced and used over and over.

Written communication, a subset of visual communication, is the foundation of all regulatory agency communication. This is because recollection of facts and details deteriorates over time. It is often said that "if it is not written down, it did not happen." The only way to ensure that something is recorded and recollected similarly by everyone is if there is documentation created at the time that supports what occurred, such as meeting minutes, study reports, deviation reports, etc.

Specifically, written communication is used to document every oral communication with an agency, including telephone calls and meetings. Of course, it is also used to provide the regulatory agency with information about studies that were conducted, results from these studies and how results should be interpreted. This chapter discusses how to create effectively written documents, with an emphasis on writing for regulatory agencies.

Chapter Objectives

- Understand the primary goals of writing.
- Discuss how the principles of writing apply to writing for regulatory agencies.
- Understand your reader and write for your reader's understanding.
- Focus and refine your writing.

Goals of Writing

Writing effectively is an art and must be practiced. Being able to write effectively will lead to better output and greater success in achieving the organization's goals. There are three primary goals of writing: entertaining, informing and persuading. Some writing attempts to achieve more than one of these goals at the same time. Writing for entertainment includes novels and magazine articles. Writing for information includes training manuals, correspondence, business development, presentations, reports and documents for regulatory agencies informing them of information about your product, such as study reports. And, writing for persuasion includes advertising, documents for decision making, presentations and documents for regulatory agency submission such as the clinical overview of the Common Technical Document (CTD).

Written communications may be formal, such as a report, professional letter or meeting minutes; semiformal, such as a presentation or business email; or informal, such as personal emails, text messages and handwritten meeting notes.

"To write well, express yourself like common people, but think like a wise man. Or, think as wise men do, but speak as common people do."
—*Aristotle, Greek philosopher*

Written communication requires more words than oral communication to ensure clarity because there is no nonverbal communication to assist and there is limited or no ability to gain feedback or ask clarifying questions. This lack of interaction is also a reason why written communication should be compelling or attention grabbing. In today's workplace, information comes from all directions. The average office worker receives many email and postal mail contacts each day. With so much information coming in, people will often stop reading something if it does not capture their interest quickly or if it is not clear how their job will benefit from thoroughly reading the information. If you are going to take the time to write something, you should make sure that it is prepared in a way that people will read it and they will remember what you have written.

To do this, it is essential that you know your readers, including their educational background, current knowledge and experience and level of understanding of your topic. In addition, you need to anticipate what your reader will want to know about the topic. Then, you must define your purpose and state it clearly. Do not prepare a document with too many objectives because this will cause confusion and misunderstanding.

Recall from Chapter 2 that there are seven Cs that apply to oral or written communication:
1. Completeness
2. Conciseness
3. Consideration
4. Clarity
5. Concreteness
6. Courtesy
7. Correctness

These seven Cs are especially important in writing because a written document endures, can be continuously referenced and is subject to verification. Therefore, make sure your writing is accurate and supported by facts (concreteness). The message must be clear and uncomplicated and the writing should avoid long, complex sentences and ideas. Complexity can muddle the main points and may lose the reader's interest, causing the message to be misunderstood and failing to get the action desired.

Here are some specific considerations related to the seven Cs when applied to written communications.

Completeness, Consideration and Courtesy

To be effective, a communication must be complete. This means it must contain all the information needed to ensure understanding of the message and to elicit the desired reaction from the reader. Since writing is meant for others to read, it is important for you to know as much as possible about your readers. Knowing your readers will help you decide what to say and how best to say it. Some readers are interested in facts and figures and others want details such as the outcomes, benefits, costs, process, sources, resources, risks, alternatives, etc., while still others want the big picture including overall impact on the project or the company and associated risks.

Consideration involves taking into account the audience's viewpoint, background, knowledge and biases so the message can be developed in such a way that readers receive it positively and understand it.

Questions to Consider About Your Readers
- Who are they?
  Do they all work in the same profession? Do they all work for the

same company? Are they a mix of management and employees? Your writing will need to be tailored for understanding by the lowest common denominator.
- What is their education level?
  Your writing will need to be targeted for understanding by readers at the lowest education level.
- What do they currently know about the topic?
  The audience's familiarity with the topic will guide your focus to the elementary, intermediate or advanced levels of your message or some variation.
- What do they need to know about the topic?
  Relative to the primary objective, what are the central points the audience needs to know? Knowing their needs will allow you to develop content to bridge the gap between what they currently know and what they ultimately need to know.
- What is their attitude toward the topic?
  Do they already have expectations about the topic? Are they positive or negative? Do you need to dispel rumors or biases before they will be ready to accept, understand or comprehend your message?

As part of understanding your reader, also refer to the section on communication flows within an organization that is discussed in Chapter 2. The writer should be courteous and respectful to the reader; consider the viewpoints of the reader and do not be judgmental or biased.

Conciseness

Conciseness means using as few words as possible to convey the message's necessary information. Concise messages are more appealing

---

Dos and Don'ts of Writing for Your Readers

Do
- Analyze your readers before you begin writing.
- Make your writing appeal to what the reader cares about most.

Don't
- Omit any important information the reader needs to know.
- Forget that the reader's attitude will influence how he or she responds to your writing.

and comprehensible to a reader. It is important to understand the purpose of the document before you begin writing. In his book *Persuasive Business Proposals: Writing to Win Customers, Clients, and Contracts,* Tom Sant explains that "you will do a better job of writing if you know what you're trying to accomplish: the *why* of a document."

Many people just sit down, begin writing and hope for the best. Sometimes they are lucky. Most likely, they will produce a poorly written or confusing document. Before you begin writing, state your purpose and how you propose to carry it out. This information should be stated briefly in one or two sentences that sum up the purpose of your writing. Next, create a brief outline.

Working in this manner does not come naturally to everyone and is a skill that requires development and refinement. I remember a primary school teacher who would require that we go through these steps and review them with her as each was completed. I had a very difficult time trying to formulate my summary sentences and an outline. I could not bring myself to think that way; I felt it was ineffective to do these things and that I was much more effective if I just began writing. However, after having written a lot of reports and other documents, I now find the opposite to be true. It is now most effective for me to prepare a summary statement and general outline with bullet points under each item on the outline and then to begin writing. After I begin writing, I can always go back and make adjustments to the initial documents, but this sets the framework for the overall document.

"If you cannot express in a sentence or two what you intend to get across, then it is not focused well enough."
— *Charles Osgood, US television commentator*

By writing one or two summary sentences before you begin the document, you can state the "why" very simply. Then, based on what you know about your reader, expand your summary sentences just enough to accomplish your intended goal and provide readers with what they need to know. Chances are, you will need to read, re-read and rewrite your document a few times to ensure it is as concise as possible while still communicating your message most effectively.

Clarity

Good writing is simple and clear. You should leave no doubt in the minds of your readers about what you are trying to say to them. Your document should focus on a specific message without cluttering the message or trying to achieve too much with the communication.

Some writers think they need big, complex words to impress a reader or lend importance to a subject. These types of words can make the subject far more complicated than it needs to be, and sometimes this causes the reader to misunderstand or lose the meaning of your writing. Choose words that are easy to read and can be understood by your target audience. Unfamiliar words and jargon cause readers to slow down or stop reading altogether.

Concreteness

A concrete message contains facts and supporting information and references. This documentation strengthens the message and the confidence the reader will have in it. When choosing references, opt for the most reliable and well-recognized sources. If there are conflicting sources, consider how or if your document will handle that. Make sure that you verify the sources that you use.

Correctness

Mistakes in your writing lessen its impact. A misspelled word, a comma in the wrong place, a period where there should be a question mark—all distract the reader from your message. The reader could infer that your writing, and perhaps your thinking, is sloppy and disorganized. Although you can use a spell-check program to catch misspelled words, it will not tell you if you are using the wrong word. There are many words in the English language that look alike or sound alike and are often confused with one another. There are also a number of words that are frequently misused. Some examples of misused words and look-alike/sound-alike words are included in Exercise 4.1.

When writing for regulatory agencies, it is especially important to use the correct words so the possibility of being misunderstood is minimized.

Another consideration when you are writing is the choice of voice and tense. Voice refers to the directness of the communication and can be active or passive. It is generally recommended that written communication use the active voice because it is clearer and more concise. However, regulatory communications, especially those coming from FDA, tend to

Written Communication

> **Exercise 4.1. Vocabulary**—In each grouping, choose the sentence that uses the word correctly. (answers at end of book)
>
> | | |
> |---|---|
> | A | 1. I did not read the report thoroughly, I only perused it. |
> | | 2. I did not read the report thoroughly, I only skimmed it. |
> | B | 1. With this presentation, we hope to affect the decision by management. |
> | | 2. With this presentation, we hope to effect the decision by management. |
> | C | 1. My supervisor complemented my organizational skills. |
> | | 2. My supervisor complimented my organizational skills. |
> | D | 1. A blood test must proceed dosing. |
> | | 2. A blood test must precede dosing. |
> | E | 1. We must insure that we have covered all possible questions. |
> | | 2. We must ensure that we have covered all possible questions. |
> | F | 1. The approval of the CTD is imminent. |
> | | 2. The approval of the CTD is eminent. |
> | G | 1. The agency placed an undue testing burden on the company. |
> | | 2. The agency placed an undo testing burden on the company. |
> | H | 1. The vials must remain stationary during their shipment. |
> | | 2. The vials must remain stationery during their shipment. |
> | I | 1. I hope you will except our invitation to participate in the study. |
> | | 2. I hope you will accept our invitation to participate in the study. |
>
> If you answered 8 or 9 correctly, you are a master of correct word usage.
> If you answered fewer than 8 correctly, make sure to review your work and look up the meaning of words that may be look-alikes or sound-alikes.

be passive. I believe this is done because passive voice depersonalizes the communication and keeps the discussion distinct from an individual.

Tense refers to writing as though it were the past, present or future. In writing for regulatory agencies, since the work has already been completed, the past tense is typically used. Future tense is used to describe actions that are being committed to or will be carried out once a product is on the market.

Another important question to address in your writing is whether to use American English or British English spelling. Your writing should consistently use one or the other. For example, using a "u" in colour is British while no "u" in color is American. However, either choice is acceptable to regulatory agencies.

In summary, an effective written communicator:
- understands her audience, the reader
- is understood in a single rapid reading by the intended audience
- puts the essential information up front
- uses correct grammar
- uses active voice
- uses a reasonably simple style with appropriate format and organization
- correctly and effectively uses facts and data to support her argument
- presents ideas in a logical fashion by stating topics, supporting arguments and conclusions

Writing Emails

Email has become a preferred way to send notes, memos and other types of communication that must arrive quickly. Email is subject to the same rules that govern other types of writing. That is, the writing should be clear and concise. Information should be presented in a compelling manner, with no mistakes in grammar, punctuation or spelling. The purpose of the email communication should be clearly stated, and the information should be written in a way that appeals to the reader.

In their book, *The Elements of Email Style: Communicate Effectively via Electronic Mail*, David Angell and Brent Heslop explain that information should be presented in short, coherent units. Readers, they say, are "turned off by large chunks of text." They also urge you to keep your language simple. "If a word confuses your readers and sends them scurrying for the dictionary, it has broken their concentration," Angell and Heslop explain. "Simple and familiar words have power." Here are a few steps to help you create professional emails:
- Always edit before you hit "send"—Take the time to proofread and edit your emails to ensure you have used good grammar, punctuation and spelling. A well-written email will make your recipient's life easier.
- Use email only when appropriate—Sometimes a face-to-face meeting or phone call might be a better approach—especially when dealing with sensitive or emotional topics.
- Do not forget to include a subject line—Using a subject line

that briefly summarizes the purpose of your email may save the recipient valuable time and help prioritize her responses.
- Keep it brief—Remember that people receive dozens, if not hundreds, of emails a day. Keep your emails short and to the point.
- Avoid using emoticons—They are inappropriate in business settings.
- Avoid using abbreviations and slang—Unless the recipient is familiar with an abbreviation, its use will just be confusing and slow communication. Additionally, text message slang (such as CU and GR8) is inappropriate in workplace communications.
- Never reply to an email in anger—Unlike face-to-face communication, it is easy to misconstrue the tone of an email. Completely innocuous comments or jokes can be taken the wrong way. If you receive an email that makes you angry or confused, take a deep breath and wait to calm down before you reply. Or better yet, talk to the individual face-to-face to address any confusion.

Regulatory Writing

Writing for regulatory agencies is subject to the same rules that govern other types of writing. It should be clear and concise with information presented in a compelling manner. And, it should be free of mistakes in grammar, punctuation and spelling. Also, keep the following rules in mind for regulatory writing:
- Stay clear of too many idioms and acronyms.
- Understand that the reader does not know what you know.
- Make sure you know what you are trying to communicate. What are your summary messages?
- Know the target audience for each section of the submission. For example, is it a technical section for a specific technical reviewer or a summary section that will be read by other disciplines as well?
- Ask a document reviewer to read the submission for understanding. Choose someone who knows little about the project and who is from the same discipline as the intended audience.

One of the primary types of documents that will be sent to regulatory agencies is the report. A report is basically an account of something that

Communication and Negotiation

happened. It is based on observation and analysis. A report gives an explanation of any circumstance, occurrence or planned operation. In a regulated environment, reports play a crucial role. Reports are required for judging a product's safety and efficacy and are ultimately the basis for regulatory product approval. An effective report can be written by following these steps:
- Determine and describe the report's objective—this is usually a restatement of the objective from the protocol for the study.
- Collect the required material (facts) for the report—this will include results listings and tables, compliance information, etc.
- Examine and evaluate the facts gathered and how best to present them.
- Prepare an outline for the report, if not already dictated.
- Draft the report and perform an edit yourself.
    o When drafting the report, make sure you describe all results reasonably and impartially.
    o Incorporate the company's key messages to the extent possible.
- Distribute the draft report to the review team and ask for feedback and recommendations (see more on this topic below).
- If possible, adjudicate the comments in a meeting with the review team so changes recommended are clear and other reviewers can voice any disagreement with changes that are being made.
- Finalize the report with all comments included.
- Conduct a final read-through of the content and have a quality check done on all facts, figures and citations included in the report.

Review and Proofread Your Document

Good writing includes extensive review, editing and proofreading. Here are some proofreading tips that may be helpful to you in general writing:
- Use spell check and grammar check on the computer.
- Do not proofread on the computer—it can be hard to spot mistakes on a screen. Instead, print a hard copy and proof it at your desk.
- Do not proofread immediately after you have finished writing. You are too close to the project and you will not see mistakes

easily. Instead, put the writing away for a day or two; then proofread it.
- Proofread three times: once for content, clarity and conciseness; a second time for grammar and punctuation; and a third to make sure you have used the correct words.
- Have others read and comment on your document. This will help not only with proofreading but also with content understanding.

Effective writing for regulatory agencies includes thorough and extensive review, editing and proofreading. It involves more than just scanning a document until you find an error. You must have reviewers critique a document's content, clarity and conciseness, as well as provide possible responses to questions that you may get from a regulatory agency so you can ensure that you have covered all topics and answered all questions prior to submission. A thorough and extensive review also makes certain that you have used proper punctuation, spelling and grammar and is a complete quality check on all facts, figures, references and citations included in the submission. If the document is submitted electronically, the review also must include a complete quality check of all bookmarks and hyperlinks within and between documents in the submission.

Improving Writing Skills

Even when you are not writing documents, there are some things you can do to continue to develop your skills as a written communicator. Here are a few ideas:
- When you read a well-written narrative, memorandum, white paper, publication or other document, ask the author or the owner of the document for a copy. Use these collected examples as a guide in the preparation of your own work.
- Put writing resources in your office or know where to find them online and use them. Minimally, you should have a grammar and style reference book, a dictionary and a thesaurus.
- Write a short article for publication in a professional journal and ask for content and editorial feedback.
- Take a writing course.

Chapter Summary

Written communication is the foundation of all regulatory agency communication. It also plays a substantial role in auditing. Remember, "if it is not written down, it did not happen." It is important to document all regulatory interactions including telephone calls and meetings as well as team meetings and other important interactions.

In addition, it is important to apply the principles of good writing to all written communications including internal documents such as standard operating procedures (SOPs) and deviation reports and all external documents such as study reports and regulatory agency summaries.

Becoming an effective regulatory writer will help improve the chances that products get approved, the company's objectives are achieved and patients receive much-needed therapies in the fastest possible way.

Chapter 4 Quiz *(Answers on page 122)*

1. True or False. Reports are critical to regulatory filings as they are required for judging the safety and efficacy of a product and are ultimately the basis for approval of products by regulatory agencies.
2. True or False. Starting your writing with summary sentences and an outline is an effective way to frame your document to make it effective.
3. "Concreteness" in writing means:
   a. The message contains facts and supportive information and references.
   b. The message uses active voice.
   c. The message uses simple style with solid vocabulary.
   d. The message presents hard, concrete ideas in a logical fashion.
4. Which of the following is not advised when writing professional email?
   a. Proofread your email before sending.
   b. Include a subject line.
   c. Keep it brief.
   d. Use emoticons, abbreviations and slang if the user is familiar with them.
5. True or False. When preparing a regulatory submission, authors should be careful to ensure the proper use of all facts, figures, references and citations in their sections so that a quality check is not required.

Communication and Negotiation

Chapter 5

Influencing and Negotiating

Introduction

We engage in influencing and negotiations every day in our personal and professional lives. Some are so frequent that we tend not to think of them in those formal terms, just everyday interactions with the people we encounter. However, whether everyday or formal, simple or complex, influencing and negotiating with other people whose interests intersect with yours are the key to success in reaching your goals.

Communicating ideas is the core of effective influencing and negotiation. Ideas give information meaning. Ideas are thoughts expressed as a sentence that is persuasive. For example, which of the following statements about what will be reviewed during a meeting would sound more interesting and persuasive?

- Profit analysis
- Profit analysis shows upturn in sales over the last year

The first choice gives attendees the facts of what will be reviewed. The second choice gives attendees the idea behind the facts and entices them to want to know more, persuading them to attend the meeting and listen attentively.

Ideas are like currency: big, small, combinable, exchangeable, losing or increasing in value. They are judged by how meaningful they are. Share them at the right time and in the right way to most effectively influence or persuade during negotiations.

"Influencing" means "the effect of one person or thing on another" and "to persuade or induce" (www.thefreedictionary.com).

"Negotiation" means "to arrange for or bring about through conference, discussion, and compromise" (Merriam Webster online) or "to confer with others to reach an agreement or arrange or settle something by mutual agreement" (Wiktionary).

Chapter Objectives
- Explain how to influence others effectively.
- Explain the negotiation process.
- Identify appropriate negotiation strategies.
- Learn how to analyze the needs of all parties involved.
- Identify the key factors that drive selection of the best negotiation strategy.

Influencing

The ability to influence others effectively is an important skill to have in life and particularly within the regulatory profession. A regulatory professional uses the skill of influencing to lead teams with or without management authority, manage submissions and gain project team or regulatory agency acceptance and agreement for appropriate regulatory actions or strategies.

The Art of Persuasion

As defined above, influencing involves persuasion. Aristotle was a master of the art of persuasion, and he outlined his thinking in his work, *Rhetoric*, where he identified three important factors: ethos, pathos and logos.

Ethos (credible) persuades people using character. If you are respectful and honest, people will be more likely to follow you because of your character. Your character convinces the follower that you are someone worth listening to.

Pathos (emotional) persuades people by appealing to their emotions. For example, when a politician wants to gain support for a bill, it often is argued, "it's for the children!" Babies, puppies and kittens abound in advertising for a reason. Although cars are neither male nor female, they are sometimes called "sexy" in commercials. Pathos allows you to tie into emotional triggers that will capture a person's attention and enlist support, but it can be easily abused, leading to a loss of ethos, as described above.

Logos (logical) persuades people by appealing to their intellect. However, remember that not everyone reacts on a rational level.

Of the three, ethos must always come first. Ideally, you want to appeal to pathos, back your arguments up with logos, and never lose ethos.

Principles of Influence

Robert B. Cialdini, PhD (a psychologist and author and scholar of influence and persuasion), said that "It is through the influence process that we generate and manage change." In his studies, he outlined five universal principles of influence, which are useful and effective in a wide range of circumstances.

1. Reciprocation—People are more willing to do something for you if you have already done something for them first. Married couples do this all the time, giving in on little things so they can ask for a spa day or an uninterrupted football game.
2. Commitment—You cannot get people to commit to you or your vision if they do not see your own commitment. Once you provide a solid, consistent example, they will feel they have to do the same.
3. Authority—If people believe you know what you are talking about and accept your expertise, they are far more likely to follow you. When people need help with something, they will seek out an authority figure. If a man in a suit and tie is standing next to a man in jeans and an old t-shirt, people will invariably ask the man with the tie for advice on a technical subject first simply because he looks like an authority.
4. Social Validation—Even if we consider ourselves independent, we love to be accepted within the group. Although you would probably say no when asked "If everyone jumped off a cliff, would you join them?" people will typically support something that is popular with their friends or peers.
5. Friendship—People listen to their friends. If they know you and like you, they are far more likely to support you. A pleasant personality can make up for a multitude of failures. More than one leader has been abandoned at the first sign of trouble because he was not very well liked.

Effective Influencing

Effective influencing involves planning, communicating and finding a solution. The key to eliciting a desired action is having engaging ideas and being persuasive.

Those who fail to plan, plan to fail. — Anonymous

Communication and Negotiation

Planning for influencing involves reviewing and strategizing around the principles reviewed above; gaining an understanding of your audience so you can develop arguments that answer the question, "What's in it for me?" and their possible objections so you can develop counter-arguments. The more complex or sensitive the issue, the more planning is required.

It is critical that you practice the principles of effective communication (refer to Chapters 3 and 4). Specifically, make sure you are clear, do not use idioms or acronyms and avoid terminology that may not be familiar to all parties or is overly complex. These factors can limit your ability to influence the listener.

Depending upon your goal for influencing, you must guide the listeners to where you want them. For example, your goal may be to cause an action, change an opinion, change a decision or find a solution. Ensure that you have credibility with the listeners, appeal to their emotions and present your argument logically. Make sure your information or presentation is in logical and easy-to-follow order so you can bring the listeners from the beginning of your idea along the path of your reasoning and around to your conclusion. Remember that you cannot hammer the idea into the minds of the listeners; you must express clear and vivid ideas that will show them why your information is correct and worthy of their support and agreement.

Following are some tactics for effective influencing you should consider while developing your discussion or presentation:

Tactic 1: Liking

People like those who like them. When you are discussing or presenting your point of view, uncover real similarities and offer genuine interest or praise. Praise charms and disarms even if it is not warranted. There must be something you can admire even in those you may dislike.

Tactic 2: Reciprocity

People repay in kind. Give to others what you want to receive, e.g., respect, honesty. Display the desired behavior you want to receive.

Tactic 3: Social Proof

People follow the lead of others similar to them. Use peer power whenever it is available. People rely heavily on cues about how to think, feel and act. Influence is often best exerted horizontally rather than vertically.

Tactic 4: Consistency

People align with clear objectives and commitments. Make your objectives active, public and voluntary to gain commitment. Write objectives down for clarity. If people feel they are coerced or pressured, they may do the opposite to express their resentment.

Tactic 5: Authority

People defer to experts. Introduce yourself and disclose your expertise; do not assume it is self-evident. Establish your expertise, specifically as it relates to the topic, prior to attempting to exert influence.

Tactic 6: Scarcity

People want more when less is available. Highlight the unique benefits and exclusive information you are sharing. Potential losses and more immediate consequences are often more impactful than potential gains or long-term consequences.

Tactic 7: Indirect Influence

People resist being told what to do and how to do it or receiving unsolicited advice. Indirect influence finds a different way to deal with anticipated or real resistance.

Tactic 7a: Modeling and Matching

Modeling is behaving in the way you want others to duplicate. Matching is generation of verbal and nonverbal behavior that matches the behavior of another person.

Tactic 7b: Acting in Accord

Acting in accord means agreeing with how the other person says you are behaving (within reason). For example, if the listener claims, "You are being condescending to me!" you can act in accord by saying, "Perhaps I did sound a bit patronizing."

Tactic 7c: Reframing

Reframing means you modify the message so it can be viewed or perceived by the receiver in a different way, thereby changing the meaning of the message. Reframing may make a message more understandable or more acceptable to the receiver. For example, if one employee has filed a sexual harassment complaint against another of your employees, you would likely interview each of them to obtain more information about the events and allegations. If the person being accused is adamant that he has done nothing wrong and closes himself off to hearing your questions or providing his recollection of events, you may be able to elicit information by indirectly influencing him through reframing; perhaps with an opening such as "you may have unintentionally discriminated against Sophia."

Tactic 7d: Paradox

Paradox is a statement that seems contradictory, unbelievable or absurd, but may actually be true. For example, if someone you know worries about deadlines, imperfections and other work for eight hours a day, to the point that he is slowing his own progress, a good piece of advice for him may be to schedule one hour per day and focus on worrying—perhaps even writing down what the worries are—and then spending the other seven hours taking care of activities that will remove items from the worry list.

Tactic 7e: Confusion

Confusion is used when you want someone to come up with her own plan, be more independent or take more initiative. When you speak in a confusing, rambling manner, people's tendency is to stop listening, go inside their minds and think things through in their own way.

Tactic 7f: The Columbo Approach

The Columbo Approach, based on the Lt. Columbo character played by Peter Falk, is the art of acting confused yourself (as opposed to causing confusion) and asking questions from a perspective of "I am not so smart, can you help me understand this?"

Tactic 7g: Storytelling and Metaphor

Tell people a story without necessarily telling them the point of the story, e.g., *The Boy Who Cried Wolf*, and allow them to draw their own conclusions.

Tactic 7h: Humor

Humor influences people to feel differently and see events from a different perspective. It puts people at ease, equalizes situations and relationships and increases creativity and group rapport.

Sometimes, the most powerful influence is not trying to influence someone. When people feel you are open to their suggestions and believe they have been heard, they will work harder even if they disagree with the methods or goals. That is the power of listening. Simply listening to others makes them feel empowered, even if you do not accept their suggestions. If followers feel there is no point talking to you, they will not, and they will disengage themselves from your vision and will only follow your directions grudgingly.

Lead and influence by example. If you are seen as making the extra effort, your followers are more likely to make the extra effort. If you hide in your office and people never see you, you will be perceived as out of the loop, uninformed and uninterested.

Negotiation

Negotiation is a method for coming to a mutual agreement or resolving disputes. It is one of the most effective ways to avoid conflicts and tensions. When individuals do not agree with one another, they sit together, discuss issues in an open forum, negotiate with one another and come to an alternative that satisfies all.

Negotiation is not hard or complicated. You just have to be clear about your expectations and interests; express them clearly, persuade the other party and come to an agreement that is acceptable to both. The techniques can be learned and practiced to make negotiators more effective.

Negotiation is important in almost all areas of life: business, personal relationships, legal procedures, government matters, etc.

Negotiation success depends upon effective communication. The other person will never know about your thoughts and ideas unless and until you share them. Just as with all communication, it is important to choose your words carefully. Do not speak just for the sake of speaking. Haphazard thoughts and abstract ideas only lead to confusion. Be crisp and precise in your speech. Refer to Chapter 4 for additional information and tips on speaking.

Types of Negotiations

Negotiation in companies takes place every day in various ways to increase output and maintain or improve relationships among employees. Some of the types of negotiation are:

Day-to-Day Negotiation

Every day we negotiate something in the workplace, either with our boss or co-workers, for the smooth flow of work.

- Negotiation between employee and boss—An employee negotiates with his boss so he is assigned responsibilities he prefers. If you are uncomfortable with an assignment that you receive, do not just accept it, rather discuss your discomfort with her. For example, if your boss wants you to prepare a report on regulatory strategies related to a potential generic competitor and generic laws are not your specialization, do not just accept the assignment because your boss has told you to do it. Discuss it with her and let her know you are not experienced in this area and you may need extra time or extra guidance; if she needs it sooner, it may be best to have someone else who might have experience in the area cover the subject. It is better to discuss and negotiate at the beginning to avoid conflicts and misunderstandings later.
- Negotiation between co-workers—Negotiation is essential among co-workers and team members to reduce the chances of disputes and conflicts. You must negotiate with your co-workers or team members and accept the tasks of which you are capable, ask for help and admit when you do not have the necessary skills or information to complete a task. Negotiation helps to increase the output of the team and eventually the organization's productivity.

Contractual Negotiation

These are negotiations to create a contract. Two parties discuss issues between them and agree on conditions acceptable to both the parties. In such cases; everything should be written. A contract is signed by both parties and both have to adhere to the contract's terms and conditions, which become legally binding. This type of negotiation is particularly important when you are dealing with vendors or potential partners. Neither an individual nor an organization can afford to spend money frivolously.

When you begin to search out a vendor or supplier, determine in advance what you require. For example, do you need a certain geographic coverage, technical knowledge, specific type of experience, breadth of services, etc. Of these factors, determine which are most important to the project's success so you will be able to judge potential vendors or suppliers according to your criteria to make the best selection.

When you are ready to create a contract, always negotiate with the vendor or supplier to try to get the most important elements for your company, for example the lowest price, the highest quality, the greatest flexibility, etc. Consider all aspects of the contract to be equally important to ensure you do not compromise your or your company's privacy, confidentiality, long-term interests, ownership, future abilities, liability and other rights and commitments. Because contracts are legally binding, it is always advisable to have a legal review and to negotiate and compromise on any points that are less than optimal for your company's interests.

Legal Negotiation

Legal negotiation takes place between an individual and a law enforcement or regulatory body. In this case, there are established rules and regulations that an individual or company must follow and the enforcement body must judge whether or not the individual or company has complied with them. Negotiations with regulatory agencies generally fall into this category.

Effective negotiation is a technique that involves motivation, process and behavior.
- Motivation—There has to be a motivation for individuals to negotiate. A motivation is a topic or the thing that is important to both parties who enter into the negotiation.
- Process—The way individuals negotiate with one another is called the process of negotiation. The process includes the various techniques and strategies employed to negotiate and reach a solution (see section below).
- Behavior—How two parties interact and communicate with one another to make their points clear during a negotiation come under behavior.

Negotiation Models

Five negotiation models are discussed below.

Win-Win Model

In this model, each individual involved in negotiation wins. Nobody loses and everyone benefits as the result of the negotiation. This is generally the preferred model of negotiation because it means that both sides come away with what they want and both are equally pleased with the outcome.

Consider the following example:

Daniel wanted to buy a laptop but it was an expensive model. He went to the outlet and negotiated with the shopkeeper to lower the price. Initially the shopkeeper was reluctant but after several rounds of discussions and persuasion, he quoted a price acceptable to him as well as to Daniel. Daniel was extremely satisfied as he could now purchase the laptop without overextending his finances. The negotiation also benefited the store owner as he could earn a profit and gain a loyal customer who might buy again in the future.

Win-Lose and Lose-Win Models

In this model one party wins and the other party loses. In such a model, after several rounds of discussions and negotiations, one party benefits while the party remains dissatisfied.

In the above example, both Daniel and the store owner benefited from the deal. Let us suppose Daniel could not even afford the price quoted by the storeowner and requested him to further lower the price. If the store owner reduced the price even more, he would not be able to earn his profit but Daniel would be very happy. Thus after the negotiation, Daniel would be satisfied but the shopkeeper would not be.

Lose-Lose Model

In this model, the outcome of negotiation is zero. No party benefits from the negotiation.

Had Daniel not purchased the laptop after several rounds of negotiation, neither he nor the store owner would have gotten anything. Daniel would have returned home empty-handed and the store owner would obviously not have earned any profit.

In this model, generally the two parties are not willing to accept one another's views and are reluctant to compromise. No discussions help.

RADPAC Model

The RADPAC Model of Negotiation is also a useful tool. Each letter in the name of this model stands for something to help with the negotiation:

R—Rapport—signifies the relationship between the parties involved in negotiation. The parties ideally should be comfortable with one another and share a good rapport.

A—Analysis—Each party must understand the other party well, including needs and interests. People must listen to each other attentively in order to hear what is behind the words, the underlying interests.

D—Debate—Nothing can be achieved without discussions of the issues and the pros and cons of ideas. The parties debate one another and each tries to convince the other.

P—Propose—Each individual proposes her best idea, trying to come up with an idea acceptable to all.

A—Agreement—Individuals come to a conclusion at this stage and if agreement has been reached, it is documented in writing for final acceptance by the parties. If agreement has not been reached and the parties decide to forego further discussion, they will move directly to closing the negotiation.

C—Close—The negotiation is complete and any agreement has been documented and executed.

Challenges to Effective Negotiation

There are few challenges to negotiation and it is important to try and overcome them.

- Unwillingness to understand the other party
  There are individuals who only think about their own interests and ignore the interests and needs of the other side.
- Lack of time
  A negotiation should never be rushed. It will take time to persuade others. Analyze carefully and only then come to a conclusion or agreement.
- Lack of preparation for the negotiation
  Do your homework before the negotiation. Do not underestimate the second party or think the other person is not as smart as you.
- Impatience
  Every individual has the right to express his views. You might not agree, but at least listen to him first to understand his views so you can persuade him.
- Criticism, sarcasm, derogatory remarks
  Never say anything that might hurt others. Remember, everyone is there to do business, so be logical and professional. Do not

become too personal or overly emotional. You should be diplomatic and intelligent for an effective negotiation.
- Last-minute changes
Both parties must be clear on what they expect from each other and stick to it. Do not change your statements or your position back and forth. Once you have reached an agreement, sign a written document in the presence of both parties.
- Rigidity
Be flexible and willing to compromise so you can find a solution that will satisfy both sides.
- Lack of confidence
Make eye contact with the person sitting on the other side of the table. It is important to be serious but at the same time be relaxed. Be straightforward and crisp in your communication.

Negotiation Skills

Nobody is born with good negotiation skills; you need time to acquire them. To negotiate effectively, an individual must learn and practice the necessary skills. Before starting a negotiation, it is important to be clear about the motivation (topic) for the negotiation. What is the objective of the negotiation? Go through as many details as you can. The second party might ask you anything and you must be prepared to allay their doubts and convince them.

Regulatory professionals in particular must know how to negotiate well to avoid conflicts, maintain relationships with team members and other co-workers, be successful with regulatory agencies, and make the organization a better place to work.

Important fundamental skills include:
- Patience—A good negotiation requires patience. Another person will not always just accept your ideas and suggestions. You need to persuade him and that may require time. Never be in a hurry to close the deal; do not rush the negotiation.
- Confidence—A professional needs to be confident enough to make his points clearly to the other party, even if they are not friendly. If you are nervous or appear desperate, the other team may take undue advantage. Be informed and prepared so you can answer expected and unexpected questions calmly. Further, confidence is impressive and can lead to a negotiating advantage.

- Control—A good negotiator must remain calm and in control even when provoked. He should never lose his temper or overreact. If you are unhappy with the deal, say so in factual terms rather than emotional ones. If the terms are not acceptable, do not keep this to yourself or assume that others will be able to read your mind and understand that something is unacceptable to you.

The Negotiation Process

Now that you are armed with the basic strategy, where do you start? Negotiation is a process. The tactics may change as the negotiation proceeds, but there are definable steps that each negotiation covers.

Planning

Conducting research and planning your strategy before the negotiation begins will give you several advantages. Thorough preparation makes it less likely you will fall victim to negotiation traps, such as arguing points that are not of interest to the other party, and ending up with less than you wanted or needed.

As with all effective communication, preparation involves knowing your audience or, in this case, the other party. Try to determine the other party's interests and needs. What will they be trying to get out of the negotiation? Where do your interests coincide with theirs? Where do your interests conflict? Remember that the other party is also there to obtain what they need or want. Do not underestimate them or make assumptions about them.

Once you have learned about the other party, re-examine your own interests. Based on what you know, are there concessions you can make that will encourage the other party to give you something that you value in return? Consider your alternative options if you do not get exactly what you want. For example, when preparing for labeling negotiations, a company typically knows what it wants to say about its product data. This is written into the requisite format and then reviewed against regulatory actions, precedent and other products in the same therapeutic class or with the same indication. Then the draft label is reviewed, taking all of this into consideration. If there are areas with which the company believes the regulatory agency may not agree, the company develops its preferred wording and alternates they can propose in the event of agency disagreement.

Communication and Negotiation

To start, write down the interests and objectives of both parties to the best of your knowledge. Make a note of which interests are common, conflicting or complementary.[1] It is important to reconcile the interests of both parties. This will help you understand and verify your assumptions about the best alternative to a negotiated agreement (BATNA) for the other party.

Remember, there is a difference between interests and positions. Interests are the underlying needs that motivate us to ask for something and are the basis for positions. Positions are the stances we take on what we want. Keep in mind that interests are not always logical or rational— and can be emotional. As a result, positions may not be logical and can be emotional as well. There can be short-term and long-term interests for both parties.

Next, identify the priorities for the negotiation. Make a list of your priorities and rank them. Make your best guess as to the other party's priorities. How well your priorities align with those of the other party will play a role in ordering each issue on the agenda. Are there items on your low-priority list that are on the other party's high-priority list? These are valuable items that you can identify as potential trade-offs, helping you position for reciprocation from the other party. Expect the opposition to also take note of their low-priority items that may be high on your list.

It is important to understand the difference between "needs" or "must-haves" (thus a higher priority) and "wants" (or lower priority), as they will provide powerful insight that can prevent unnecessary bargaining. If both lists have the same high-priority items, develop alternative solutions before starting the negotiation.

Determine the BATNA for both parties. If an alternative is available, even if it is not optimal, the negotiator is less likely to accept a bad deal. Correspondingly, if the BATNA is highly undesirable, the motivation to stay at the negotiating table to find a solution will be greater. Whoever has the stronger BATNA has the stronger negotiating position. Circumstances that require negotiation with regulatory agencies are more specialized than those encountered in the broader world. The goal of regulatory agencies is the protection of public health, but that does not preclude other factors from entering into the negotiation, such as interpretation of the law and unmet medical needs of patients. The circumstances that require the negotiation can be very different (e.g., negotiating the labeling for final product approval is different from agreeing on the appropriate corrective actions after a severe Warning Letter). This can lead to a different BATNA for both sides.

If the other party's BATNA is weaker than yours, avoid getting greedy. Win-win scenarios are generally the best solution when dealing with regulatory issues, whether you are negotiating with a regulatory agency or within your own organization. After all, you are likely to be involved in future negotiations with these same people. Finding a win-win solution when you are in a position to force the other party into a win-lose situation could generate good will that might serve you well in the future.

Next, identify the limits of authority granted to the negotiators. If there are significant issues on the interest list that exceed the authority of the assigned negotiators, consider what actions should be taken if this limit is reached. This means understanding not only the limits of authority for the other party but your own authority limits as well. If either party exceeds the limits of its authority, it can delay resolution and damage the confidence of both parties.

Additionally, plan an agenda that lists the issues in the sequence you wish to discuss them. If possible, use an agenda you have created. It will give you the ability to better control the process. When planning your agenda, allocate time for discussion based on the number of anticipated contentious issues. Remember, it takes time to persuade the opposition on contentious issues. If you must use the opposing party's agenda, study it carefully to discern priorities or strategies.

Assign a time limit for each agenda item to better manage the flow of the discussions and prevent getting "stuck" on one issue. It may be beneficial to reach agreement on the simple issues first. These are the issues that are low priority for one party and high priority for the other. This approach allows both sides to achieve "victories" early in the negotiation and can build confidence on both sides, increasing the trust needed to obtain a mutually beneficial agreement on the higher-priority issues later in the process.

Communicating

Communicating is critical during the negotiation process. In this stage, you will test the assumptions about the other party's interests and priorities you made during the planning stage. Each party's interests and priorities should be explored and clarified. If the other party does not seem willing to reveal their interests and priorities, probe them with questions and listen carefully so you can determine whether their interests are

Communication and Negotiation

what you believed they would be during your planning. Changes in style or approach may be needed as each party's interests become clearer.

You should also use this stage as an opportunity to build trust. Set procedural rules or criteria to follow during the negotiation. When everyone agrees to a set of rules, people are less likely to feel "taken" or cheated at the end of the negotiation.

Use general questions first to identify general needs, wants and concerns—check them against your assumptions. Do not use leading or rhetorical questions. Avoid questions that are accusatory or threatening.

During the negotiation, be clear in your communication (refer to Chapter 2 for more details on effective communication). Make sure the purpose of the negotiation is clear. Stay consistent on your position. Do not be in a confused state of mind yourself, and do not change your statements or play with words to cause confusion. Do not accept a compromise during a negotiation that will leave you in a worse position than if you reached no agreement. You will know what these positions are if you have considered your plans and your alternatives.

Be an effective listener (see Chapter 2). Do not jump to conclusions; listen to what the other party offers and give it consideration. Achieving what you want will require some compromise. An exchange of what they want for what you want, with neither of you suffering a huge loss, is the deal that you should both be seeking. If you have done your preparation, you will understand the other party's situation well and will know when to compromise.

Stay focused during the negotiation. Be clear about what you want and ask for it. Do not expect the other party to be able to read your mind. And, do not assume they have come as prepared as you (but do not assume they are unprepared, either). Be realistic in what you request. Do not ask for something you know is going to be impossible.

The words you use are critical. Choose words that can persuade—either for or against your position—and avoid using negative words that can shut down the negotiation process. During your planning stage, rehearse the words you will use in your communication.

Follow the usual rules of respect and stay professional. Be on time for the negotiation. Be honest; do not fake anything or manipulate the truth. Do not use foul or abusive language. Do not insult anyone. Maintain control of your emotions and do not become angry or upset.

Nonverbal communication also plays an important role in an effective negotiation. Facial expressions, hand movements and posture matter a lot and must not be ignored. You must also be careful with the pitch and tone of your voice. You are more likely to be successful if you are calm and polite. Do not be rude or short-tempered with others. Do not speak either too quickly or too slowly. The other person must understand your speech. Speak in a tone that can be heard by everyone, but do not be loud or shout. Sit straight; do not lean on the chair. Make eye contact with the other party. Do not play with things on the table.

If you are speaking to someone who is nervous, sweating unnecessarily and moving things around, what would you think about this person? Would you think he is confident in his speaking or in his position? If you behave in a similar manner, the other party would likely have the same reaction. If they see that you are nervous, they probably will try to take advantage of you. Instead, be very confident and show a positive attitude. Smile, but do not laugh unnecessarily or crack silly jokes. Exchange greetings and compliments. Concentrate on the negotiation.

Developing Solutions

Based on the information gathered from your research and understanding of the interests of both parties, outline the options you will propose first. Practice defending your first offer. Be able to clearly explain why your offer will satisfy the other party's needs. Also determine the best possible agreement (BPA) and the minimal possible agreement (MPA). With these clearly in mind, the boundaries and alternatives of the negotiation should be well defined.

To reach an agreement, proposals must be made. Brainstorm acceptable options with the other party. Listen carefully to what is said by the other side. Keep your BATNA, MPA and BPA in mind as discussions proceed.

As concessions are offered and tentative agreements reached, keep track of each one. Remember that proposals are just that—proposals. Until all issues are addressed, it is possible that one issue later in the negotiation will trigger a change to a point on which agreement was previously reached. Proposals allow the negotiators the flexibility to emphasize a shared consensus and move closer to an agreement.

Closing

Take your time during the discussion and in coming to an agreement. Once you have reached an agreement, do not drag out the conversation any longer. Close the deal.

Confirm exactly what has been agreed to on both sides. Capture these points on paper. Pay careful attention to the words to avoid ambiguity. Use what you have learned in earlier chapters to clearly communicate the agreement. Any misunderstandings are easier to resolve during closing than after the negotiation has ended. The written words must communicate the same message in the days and weeks to come. The terms of the agreement should be clear to all parties, even those who were not directly involved in the negotiation process.

Make sure you review all of the paperwork and documents associated with the deal. Do not sign anything with which you do not agree. Make sure all of the points of agreement are stated clearly and in sufficient detail according to the agreed terms.

Negotiation Styles

Everyone has a negotiation style with which they are most comfortable, but the same style cannot be used for every situation. It is important to understand your own style as well as to identify the styles of others. Be alert to style changes that occur during the negotiation. The same style that is effective at the beginning of a negotiation may not be successful in later discussions. Successful negotiators learn to recognize what style best fits a situation and adapt accordingly.

Negotiation styles can be broken down into five different types:[2]

1. Collaboration

Collaborators prefer finding solutions by working with the opponent to solve the problem. Their perspective is that by teaming up with the opposition, they can find a solution that will be a win-win. In other words, it is "us against the problem," not "us against them."

2. Accommodation

Accommodators focus their attention on solving the opponent's problems. They place a high value on the personal relationship with the opponent. They often make concessions to the opposition for the sake of preserving the relationship. As long as the opposing party also employs an accommodation or a compromise position, a win-win scenario is possible. However, if the other side employs a different position, the accommodator may be in a lose position.

3. Competition

This style is characterized by a love of conflict. Any concession is viewed as losing and competitors do not like to lose. Their perspective is that their opponent must lose, resulting in a win-lose or a lose-lose solution.

4. Conflict Avoidance

Conflict avoiders are the opposite of competitors. These negotiators actively avoid disagreement and seek to resolve differences in peace and quiet. Depending upon the opposition, this approach may result in a win or lose for either side.

5. Compromise

Interested in fairness, compromise negotiators will tend to "split the difference" and resolve the back-and-forth bargaining. As long as the opposing party also employs a compromise or accommodation position, this strategy may result in a win-win scenario. However, if the other side employs a different position, the compromiser may be in a lose position.

Difficult Tactics

You have done your homework and are thoroughly prepared for the negotiation. You have identified the BATNA, MPA and BPA for both yourself and the other party. They, however, are being "difficult." There are several tactics or behaviors that make a negotiation more difficult to complete. There are five common types of difficult negotiators, which are variations on the negotiation styles that were previously discussed. These types are known as the haggler, the re-visitor, the debater, the extremist, the "this-or-nothing" negotiator and the non-reciprocator.

When faced with difficult tactics or difficult individuals, focus on your BATNA and your preparation. Each difficult tactic is used to encourage a deviation from your plan and can trigger emotional responses, both of which can stall the negotiation and undermine its effectiveness. The only things you are able to truly control are your responses and reactions. Understanding your feelings and sensitivities will allow you to adjust your response to those using difficult tactics.

Humor, when appropriate, can be helpful in dealing with a difficult opponent. Caution should be exercised because you could indirectly insult the other party either personally or professionally. If you feel a situation is overly tense, take a break. If possible, sleep on it, regroup and come back with fresh thoughts.

Remember that the tactics the other party is using have a specific purpose: to gain an advantage in the negotiation. By learning to recognize difficult tactics and to avoid falling into potential traps, you can move past these barriers to gain a resolution to the issues at hand. You can also learn when it is to your advantage to implement them yourself.

Chapter Summary

Thorough planning is needed in both influencing and negotiation processes to avoid unnecessary or irrelevant distractions and to persuade others. The more complex the issue, the more planning is likely to be required.

There are many details to keep in mind during the negotiation process. While it may seem overwhelming at first, planning thoroughly and following the steps outlined here should get you through successfully. Everyone negotiates every day. It is likely you already know how to identify the styles of the opposition and the difficult tactics that they may employ.

References and Resources
1. Cohen S. "Negotiation is not a competitive sport." Ivey Management Services. 2004.
2. Mills H. *The StreetSmart Negotiator: How to Outwit, Outmaneuver, and Outlast Your Opponents.* AMACOM. 2005.

Additional Resources
Tingley J. *The Power of Indirect Influence.* AMACOM, 2000
Cialdini R. "Harnessing the Science of Persuasion." Harvard Business Rreview. 3/3/2009
Gardner H. *Changing Minds: The Art and Science of Changing our Own and Other People's Minds.* Harvard Business Press. 2004.

Negotiating and Influencing

Chapter 5 Quiz (Answers on page 122)

1. What does BATNA stand for?
   a. Best agreement to be negotiated and agreed
   b. Best alternative to a negotiated agreement
   c. Best actions turned to negotiated agreement
   d. None of the above
2. Which of the following is a challenge to an effective negotiation?
   a. Taking too much time
   b. Lack of confidence
   c. Being too flexible
   d. Both a and b
3. Which of the following negotiation styles focuses on solving the opponent's problems and make concessions for the sake of preserving the relationship?
   a. Collaboration
   b. Accommodation
   c. Competition
   d. Conflict avoidance
   e. Compromise
4. In the RADPAC model of communication, each letter stands for something. R is rapport, A is analysis, D is_____, P is propose, A is agreement and C is close.
   a. Discuss
   b. Discover
   c. Debate
5. True or False. Effective communication is important for good negotiation.

Communication and Negotiation

Chapter 6

Global Business Etiquette and Cultural Considerations

Introduction

Effective communicators must be aware of how the other party receives a message, interprets it and responds or reacts to it. Increased communication in today's Internet age has led to more intercultural communication than ever before. People talk and communicate across states, countries, cultures and religions. While technology has made communication faster and easier, it is important that intercultural communication be handled with sensitivity.

People interpret messages based on their values, beliefs, culture and assumptions. This could lead to misunderstanding unless the communicators are aware of potential pitfalls and complete background research on the individual or group or the country where the business will be conducted.

Chapter Objectives

- Describe the importance of cultural considerations in communication.
- Describe a strategy to research cultural matters.
- Show how some cultural differences impact communication on key issues.

Cultural Awareness

Our biases and prejudices are deeply rooted within us. From the moment we are born, we learn about ourselves, our environment and the world. Families, friends, peers, books, teachers, idols and others influence our opinions on what is right and what is wrong. Early learning shapes our perceptions about how we view things and respond to them. What we learn and experience gives us a subjective point of view known as a bias. Our biases serve as filtering lenses that allow us to make sense of new information and experiences based on what we already know. Many of our biases are good because they allow us to believe that something is true without concrete evidence. Otherwise, we would have to start learning anew in everything that we do. But, if we allow our biases to shade our perceptions of people and what they are capable of, they are potentially harmful. We begin to pre-judge others on what we think they can or cannot do or understand and how we think they will react.

Training in diversity will not erase these biases and deeply rooted beliefs. However, development and training can help us to become aware of our own biases and beliefs so that we can make a conscious effort to not pre-judge others and to be more open-minded in communication. Fully embracing diversity is more than tolerating or understanding people who are different. It means actively welcoming and involving them in the company and in communication.

Diversity in an Organization

Organizations need a diverse group of people on every team so that they can be productive. Diversity is not only black and white, female and male, homosexual and heterosexual, Jew and Christian, young and old, etc., but is also the uniqueness of every individual, for example, slow learner and fast learner, introvert and extrovert, scholar and sports person, liberal and conservative, thinker and dreamer. It takes a wide variety of people for a team and a company to become the best. Embracing diversity means understanding, valuing and positively using the differences in every person. It empowers people and makes an organization more effective by capitalizing on the strengths of each employee. Team members must develop the ability to rely on all their teammates, no matter how different they may be.

To be successful, an organization or a team needs team builders, thinkers, dreamers, organizers, controllers, doers and so on, to reach the goals that can make it the best. If an organization had only a group of team builders, it would get nowhere because everyone would be continuously trying to create teams, while a group of doers will all be trying to accomplish something without a clear, unified goal or vision to guide them.

To obtain that competitive edge, you need to grow your groups into teams that use the full potential of every individual. When grown into a team (refer to Chapter 2 for additional information on teams), the members understand and support one another. Their main goal is to see the team accomplish its mission. Failing to accept others for what and who they are and failing to realize that diversity is the key for turning weak areas into strong areas will cause the team to perform suboptimally and potentially fail. However, if the team accepts differences and uses the strengths of every individual, it will create a synergy that will get more out of every effort and create a competitive advantage over other teams or organizations where people act alone.

Intercultural Communication Across an Organization

There are basic differences across multicultural teams that can cause communication issues, whether members are all located together or are working from different locations. Communication in the workplace becomes even more critical in these circumstances as you need to carefully consider the way culture affects how a message is delivered, how it is heard, how it is understood, and how this impacts team dynamics and processes.

Here are some tips for effective communication within multicultural teams:

- Discuss with team members their possible cultural differences.
- Establish how these cultural differences may affect interactions and performance.
- Factor differences (e.g., time zones, holidays, availability of technology, decision-making process, work hours, etc.) into any team processes that may be affected, such as review periods, meetings and response times.
- Discuss how these differences may potentially affect team norms, the exchange of information, decision making and communications.
- Discuss tools and techniques for overcoming all potential barriers that have been identified.
- Gain team member agreement for sensitivities to cultural differences and for implementing appropriate tools and techniques to respect the input and involvement of all team members.

In summary, effective communication in the workplace requires that clear goals be established for teams and that team members continuously and openly communicate with one another and with management. Communication within the team will form naturally as individuals collaborate; this process should be nurtured through regular team interactions.

Communication and Negotiation

Intercultural Communication Outside an Organization

Just as organizations are becoming more diverse internally, they are also becoming more cross-culturally diverse in their customer base and contractor and partner selections. As with internal communication, basic cultural differences can cause communication issues with external audiences. It is important for the success of these relationships to consider how culture will affect the communications and team processes.

Additionally, you may be asked to travel internationally, deliver a presentation to a global or culturally diverse audience or present to a domestic audience from another country. To make sure there is no misunderstanding, it is important to research the culture of the individual or group with whom you will be communicating.

Conduct Research

An important part of communicating effectively is being aware of how the other party will receive, understand and respond to your message. Therefore, before communicating with others in another nation or region, you should research their cultural norms, etiquette and expectations. Specifically, it is recommended that you research the following topics:

- holidays
- suitable business or formal attire
- gift-giving practices
- business hours
- acceptable subjects of conversation
- greeting practices
- meeting formalities and acceptable venues
- formality of speech and words used
- time sensitivities
- body language
- other aspects of etiquette

Here are some examples of what you might find.

Business Card Etiquette

- Middle East—Present your card with your right hand, never your left.
- China—Have one side of the card translated into Chinese using gold-colored lettering as that color is auspicious; offer the card

Global Business Etiquette and Cultural Considerations

- with both hands.
- Japan—Very ceremonial; status is important; job title should be prominent; give the card with one hand, but accept with two hands and examine it for a few moments, then comment about it; carefully place the card on the table in front of you for the duration of the meeting. Writing on a business card is seen as impolite.
- India—Education is important so make sure degrees are displayed on the card; offer the card with the right hand only.
- Madagascar—Be sure not to use red ink on your business cards. The color red has a negative connotation in this country.

Holidays
- Scandinavia—It is both difficult and inconsiderate to try to conduct major business deals during July and August as many companies close for extended periods during these months so employees can go on holiday.
- Guatemala—Here, as well as in most of Latin America, little to no business is conducted during Holy Week (the week leading up to Easter).
- US—It is difficult to conduct business during the period between Christmas (December 25) and New Year's Day (January 1) because many businesses shut down and in others many employees take vacation.

Professional Titles
- Ireland—Professional titles are not prevalent and are usually seen as arrogant.
- Czech Republic—Ensure that you learn the titles of everyone you have meetings with as these distinctions are extremely important in this culture.

Greeting
- Russia—Shaking hands through a doorway is considered bad luck and should be avoided.
- West Africa—It is important not to shake hands or pass anything with your left hand, as this hand is used for hygiene purposes only.
- Kenya—Business people of the same sex who are well acquainted

may greet each other with hugs. Wait for your Kenyan counterpart to initiate this action.
- South Africa—The peace sign, formed by extending the index and middle fingers with the palm facing towards your body, is considered extremely rude.
- US—It is customary for both men and women to shake hands firmly in greeting.

Gift-giving and Receiving
- China—Individuals may refuse a gift multiple times before finally accepting it. Make it known that the gift is from your company. If you receive a gift, it is advisable to express appreciation upon receipt.
- Bahrain—If you compliment someone on a personal item, they may insist that you accept it as a gift.

Body Language
- India—Shaking one's head from side to side signals agreement and interest in what is being said or expressed. It does not suggest disagreement or disapproval.
- South Korea—A "yes" answer is often an acknowledgement of something being discussed or conveyed, and does not necessarily mean agreement.
- Saudi Arabia—A man, as a sign of friendship, may hold hands with another man in certain social settings.
- Venezuela—Once you establish a relationship with certain people, you may receive an "abrazo," which is a customary embrace that may be accompanied by a kiss on the cheek.

Other Common Practices and Etiquette
- Qatar—Sample all of the food that your Qatari colleague serves at a meal; this shows respect.
- Middle East—The first part of a business meeting is almost invariably reserved for your Middle Eastern associate to become acquainted with you (and vice versa). It is common to have discussions about global events, politics or religion. In some cases, it may be considered rude to launch into a business discussion or negotiation without first engaging in a conversation about these unrelated topics. In fact, these

Global Business Etiquette and Cultural Considerations

conversations may prove critical in establishing a business relationship.
- Kuwait—During meetings, there may be a man who appears to be part of the business delegation, but whose sole job is to offer and serve coffee. Try not to take too much notice, as he will not be a participant in your business discussions or transactions. His service role merely reflects the Middle Eastern custom of offering guests refreshments.
- Colombia—It may be considered an insult to leave immediately after a meeting is completed, as doing so may suggest that you are not interested in getting to know your counterparts.
- Mexico—Conversations occur at a much closer physical proximity than in most other countries. Moving away to establish distance is considered unfriendly. In response, your counterpart may step toward you to close the distance.
- US—It is considered inappropriate to discuss religion or politics in the business setting.

General Intercultural Communication Strategies

In addition to doing specific research, you should keep some general rules in mind when communicating interculturally:
- Do not use slang or idioms (e.g., "raining cats and dogs" to mean "raining a lot").
- Choose specific and relevant words that are simple.
- Be an attentive listener.
- Check for understanding.
- Ask questions if there is any doubt.
- Understand the importance of intonation while communicating. Stress on a specific word can change the entire meaning of a sentence. For example:
    "I never said HE stole the money" vs.
    "I never said he STOLE the money"
  The first sentence stresses "HE," meaning that someone else may have stolen the money. The second sentence stresses "STOLE," meaning that the money may not have been stolen but may have disappeared by another means.
- Check your body language/gestures. Some cultures might find a particular gesture offensive.
- Know the comfortable level of eye contact and distance between

two people while making a formal vs. informal communication.

Cross-cultural Negotiations

Cross-cultural negotiations can be particularly tricky. The same rules apply as in any other type of negotiation, but with the added difficulties posed by a different language or a different preferred style of communication. It is very important to understand the people with whom you are negotiating. What is the history of their organization or country? What are the differences in manners or courtesies? Care must be taken to avoid inadvertently insulting your opposition.

As discussed in Chapter 5, when you are planning the negotiation, it is critical that you understand the opposition's priorities as they relate to their BATNA, BPA and MPA. Without understanding the people involved in the negotiation, you cannot be fully prepared. The greater your understanding of your opposition, the better you will be able to explain your position to them and understand theirs.

Keep an open mind. Be willing to recognize the assumptions you have made while planning and adjust them if they were incorrect or if the situation changes during the negotiation. Your preparations, no matter how thorough, may have missed something.

Unfortunately, there is no magic formula for negotiation because it is always subject to dynamic change. Understand the tactics available to you and use them as you would tools from a toolbox. Select the tools you need that best fit the job at hand and employ them to the best of your ability for a successful outcome.

Clear communications are a critical factor for negotiation. Because of language differences, preparation of written agendas and meeting minutes give all parties a chance to take time in interpreting and understanding the exchanges.

Chapter Summary

Conducting research and fully understanding the cultural norms and expectations of other parties that will participate in a communication are critical to ensuring its effectiveness. Understanding their culture will go a long way toward making your intercultural communication and negotiation effective.

Global Business Etiquette and Cultural Considerations

Chapter 6 Quiz (*Answers on page 122*)

1. True or False. It is important to conduct research into the country and culture of the people with whom you are communicating.
2. Which of the following topics are important to research for cultural differences?
   a. Business hours and holidays
   b. Greetings and meeting expectations
   c. Body language and attire
   d. All of the above
3. When communicating cross culturally, which of the following statements is FALSE?
   a. Different rules apply than when you communicate within the same culture and communication must be approached from a different perspective.
   b. You should not use slang or idioms.
   c. You should be an attentive listener.
4. Which of the following statements about multicultural teams is TRUE?
   a. Team members should discuss their cultural differences.
   b. Team members should establish the team culture and all members must erase their cultural beliefs for the sake of the team.
   c. Team members in different time zones should do all work according to the time zone where the leader is located.
5. True or False. When exchanging business cards, always place those cards you receive into your pocket immediately.

References and Resources

Explore the following references and resources to learn more about understanding cultural differences and negotiating and communicating effectively across cultures both within an organization and with external affiliates, partners, or regulatory agencies.

- Cohen S. "Negotiation is not a competitive sport," *Ivey Business Journal*, July/August 2004.
- Ionescu R. *Influencing for Results* website, www.negotiations.com/articles/negotiation-techniques.
- Lum G. *The Negotiation Fieldbook*, McGraw-Hill, 2005.
- Mills H. *The Streetsmart Negotiator*, American Management

Association, 2005.
- The Negotiation Experts website, www.negotiations.com/.
- The Negotiation Skills Company Inc. website, www.negotiationskills.com/articles.php.
- Executive Planet, www.executiveplanet.com.
- Business Etiquette Around the World, www.cyborlink.com.
- Cultural Savvy, www.culturalsavvy.com.
- International Addresses and Salutations, www.bspage.com/address.html.
- Arabian Business and Cultural Guide, www.traderscity.com/abcg.
- Business Japan, www.gate39.com/business/default.aspx.
- Sweden: Industry and Trade Information, www.sverigeturism.se/smorgasbord/smorgasbord/industry.
- Cultural Interviews with Latin American Executives, www.laits.utexas.edu/~orkelm/laexec/laexec.html.

Exercise and Quiz Answers

Chapter 1
Exercise 1.1 Writing for the Target Audience.
Desired outcome: My desired outcome would be to have the students see my passion about this career and give them an understanding of its importance in the world so they may be interested in pursuing a regulatory career. I also want to tell them where to find more information.

Target audience and shaping the message: The target audience is a group of 17-to 19-year-old high school students. Their primary interests will be the opposite sex, parties, cars, nice clothes, friends, acceptance, looks, popularity and similar things. Their vocabulary, while somewhat developed, is unlikely to include "regulatory affairs" or "pharmaceutical." And, they are probably only attending career day because they have been required to do so, not because they actually expect to hear anything remotely interesting.

Achieving the desired outcome: To achieve the desired outcome in five to seven minutes, it will be critically important to grab the attention of the audience within the first 15 seconds, spend the next 60 seconds engaging them and then engrossing them in the topic so that after five minutes, they believe it is actually a pretty cool thing to do and they might be interested in getting more information so they make a note on their book cover or in their smart phone.

First two minutes: Good morning everyone. Thank you for inviting me to speak to you today. I am here to tell you about the best career in the world—how to sell drugs and not get into trouble. That's right. This is what I do for a living. I work for a company called BrilliancePharma. We make drugs that help people get well, live better lives, look better and feel better. In order to make sure these people hear about our drugs, we have to advertise them for sale. How many of you have seen a drug advertised on TV or in a magazine or on a billboard or the Internet? [pause for hands] What is one of the ads that you remember seeing? [pause for response; e.g., Viagra, Cialis, Advair, etc.] What caught your attention about the ad? [pause for response, e.g., messages, images, implications, etc.] And, have you ever listened to the part of the advertisement that lists reactions or says to talk to your doctor? What do you remember about that? [pause for response] Well, the next time you listen to an ad, think about the fact that every advertisement for a prescription drug that is aired on TV has to meet US Food and Drug Administration laws and standards. Every word spoken and every word and image that appears on the screen has to be reviewed by a team of people to make sure the drugs will sell and the company will not get into trouble for what they say. I have been helping to make drugs available to the people who need them for more than 10 years. I love coming to work every day and knowing that the drugs I work on have helped millions of people live better lives. You can help them too. If you are interested in a career like mine, visit the website RAPS.org and search for information about careers.

Chapter 1 Quiz
Answers:
1. False
2. a
3. True
4. Any three of the following: noise, unorganized or disorganized thought, wrong interpretations, not understanding the receiver, ignoring the content, avoiding the listener or receiver, not confirming with the receiver, low pitch and tone, impatient listener, or an individual's barriers
5. d

Chapter 2
Exercise 2.1 Listening Skills
Answers:
1. False
2. False
3. True
4. True
5. False

Chapter 2 Quiz
Answers:
1. True
2. b
3. True
4. c
5. d

Chapter 3
Exercise 3.1 Clarifying Questions
Answers:
1. b
2. a
3. a
4. b
5. a
6. b
7. a
8. b
9. a

Chapter 3 Quiz
Answers:
1. True
2. d
3. True
4. False
5. b

Chapter 4
Exercise 4.1 Vocabulary
Answers:
A. 2
B. 1
C. 2
D. 2
E. 2
F. 1
G. 1

Communication and Negotiation

H. 1
I. 2

Chapter 4 Quiz
Answers:
1. True
2. True
3. a
4. d
5. False

Chapter 5
Chapter 5 Quiz
Answers:
1. b
2. b
3. b
4. c
5. True

Chapter 6
Chapter 6 Quiz
Answers:
1. True
2. d
3. a
4. a
5. False